To my father,

Richard W. Benson

*But now ask the beasts, and they will teach you;*
*And the birds of the air, and they will tell you;*
*— Job 12:7*

D.B.

To all of my friends who have joined me in the field
and helped me find the woodpeckers,

especially Rosa Duarte, Pam and Keith Kingdon, Jamie Acker, and Brady Beck

P.B.

Stone Ridge Press
2515 Garthus Road
Wrenshall, MN 55797
www.StoneRidgePress.com
thesparkygroup@gmail.com

BIRD NERD NATURAL HISTORY
WOODPECKERS OF NORTH AMERICA:
A NATURALIST'S HANDBOOK

Printed in South Korea by Doosan
10  9  8  7  6  5  4  3  2  1   First Edition


Graphic Designer: Mark Sparky Stensaas
Maps by Matt Kania (www.MapHero.com)
Cover Photos by Paul Bannick (www.PaulBannick.com)


ISBN-13:  978-09760313-7-6  softcover

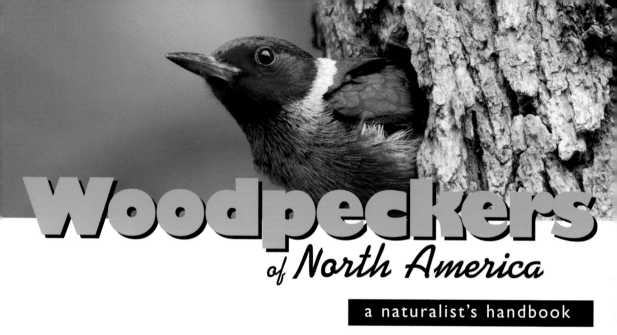

# Woodpeckers
### of *North America*

## a naturalist's handbook

by David Benson
Photographs by Paul Bannick

Stone Ridge Press

# Acknowledgments

Long ago, when I was teaching English as a Second Language, I told one of my international students of my interest in birds. She looked at me, wide-eyed, and shuddered, "Oh, I hate birds!" I was shocked and figured there must have been some linguistic confusion at the root of such an outrageous statement. Further questioning only clarified that she did indeed hate birds, and she hated them categorically. It became obvious that she was just as shocked at my statement as I was at hers!

I have never met anyone else who admitted to such a thing. In fact, I have had the pleasure of many friends and field companions who love birds seemingly without reservation. I am grateful to all of them, with special thanks to Jonas Benson, Lars Benson, Pamela Benson, Kim Eckert, Alexander Ellis, Jesse Ellis, John Ellis, Dave Grosshuesch, John Heid, Mike Hendrickson, Jim Lind, Frank and Kate Nicoletti, Jan Shaffer and Dr. Thomas W. Shaffer, Dave Steininger, Sparky Stensaas, Paul Sundberg, Peder Svingen, Suzanne Swanson, Bill Tefft, Erik Torch, Sandra van den Bosse, Larry Weber, Sue Weber, Lori Williams, and Ben Yokel.

I owe a debt to all of the authors listed in the bibliography (and beyond them, hundreds more who are listed in their bibliographies). I am grateful to have my ideas appear between the covers of a book with the splendid photography of Paul Bannick.

Even greater thanks to Sparky Stensaas, the publisher of this book, for his perseverance, curiosity, skill, and friendship.

David Benson,

Duluth, Minnesota
March 2014

# Table of Contents

Map Key
■ Breeding
■ Winter
■ Year-round

# Sidebar Essays

# Lewis's Woodpecker

*Description* Greenish head and back, dark red face, gray color and breast, pinkish belly; despite all of these colors, may look like a crow at first glance—dark cast to plumage

*Juveniles* Lack the gray collar; head and back are deep brown, little red on the face, with some streaking and barring on the underparts

*Length* 10.5 inches

*Wingspan* 21 inches

*Range* From southern British Columbia and Alberta south through entire Great Basin

*Other Names* *Melanerpes lewis* (Scientific)
*Pic de Lewis* (French)
*Carpintero de Lewis* (Spanish)

This is one of my favorite birds, possibly because it took me so long to finally find one! Having searched fruitlessly at several places in the West, I got to see my first at a bird feeder in Roosevelt, Minnesota, a small town on the Canadian border. It stayed there for several weeks, and many Minnesota birders made the pilgrimage to add it to their state lists. Even though it is in the genus *Melanerpes* with several other species, it is truly an unusual woodpecker.

## Identification

A big, dark woodpecker with wide, rounded wings and buoyant flight.

Greenish-black head and back, deep red face, pearly gray breast patch extending around the neck like a collar, and pinkish red belly; sexes are alike.

Unmistakable with a good look; at a glance, might be dismissed as just another crow flying by—big dark bird with direct, rowing flight; not undulating like many woodpeckers.

## Sounds

Often silent, but call note is a weak *cheef*, or a descending series of several squeaks; rattling, starling-like roll.

Drum is short, soft, medium-speed roll, followed by taps.

## Habitat

Ponderosa Pine forest with an open canopy, Cottonwood riverlands, or logged or burned pine forest.

## Range

Southern British Columbia and Alberta south through entire Great Basin, uncommon throughout most of its range.

# Types of Holes

All woodpeckers excavate holes—mostly in trees, but also in cacti and other plants, or in wood on a structure. One can usually tell if a hole in a tree is made by a woodpecker, but the holes of most species are tough to separate unless you are watching the bird make the hole. Two exceptions are the holes of Pileated Woodpeckers, which are large and slightly squared at the corners; and the holes made by the sapsucker species, which are small and made in regular rows and lines that may cover large areas on a tree. Nesting woodpeckers usually make holes only large enough as they need to be, so the cavity of a small woodpecker would not be large enough to admit a large one.

1. Williamson's Sapsucker sap wells on pine.
2. Gila Woodpecker cavity in Saguaro cactus.
3. Rectangular excavation holes of Pileated.
4. Yellow-bellied Sapsucker sap wells on birch.

## Food

Insects and other arthropods, nuts, and fruits; chops up acorns in fall and caches them. Diet varies with the season—eats more acorns during the fall and fruit during the winter; mainly eats flying insects during the summer. Eats grit during acorn season, presumably to help with digestion.

## Behavior Notes

This woodpecker is known for agile, swallow-like flight, which it displays when fly-catching from perches, one of its preferred methods of hunting during summer.

Some are permanent residents, but there is an annual movement to lower elevations; all individuals in the northern parts of the range move south in winter, but not a long-distance migrant. Some years, large numbers are seen in the lowlands of the southwest in winter. It is always local and variable, so population numbers are hard to assess.

Like Red-headed, Black-backed and American Three-toed Woodpeckers, Lewis's is a fire follower, opportunistically hunting and eating in burned over areas.

Pairs may mate for life and re-use a nest site.

Nest cavity is made in a tree or pole, from five to 100+ feet off the ground.

Eggs are white; average clutch size is five to seven.

1. Juvenile plumage is quite drab compared to adults.

2. Lewis's searching for acorns in a fall oak.

# Meriwether Lewis's Bird

This species was named for Meriwether Lewis, co-leader of the Lewis and Clark Expedition of 1804-1806, who first mentioned the bird in English. The name was given by Alexander Wilson, who included the species in his writing based on Lewis's collected skins.

*May 27th, 1806*

*The black woodpecker which I have frequently mentioned and which is found in most parts of the Rocky Mountains as well as the Western and S. W. mountains. I had never an opportunity of examining until a few days since when we killed and preserved several of them. …around the base of the beak including the eye and a small part of the throat is of a fine crimson red. …the neck and as low as the crop in front is of an iron grey. …the belly and breast is a curious mixture of white and blood red which has much the appearance of having been artificially painted or stained of that color.*

*~ Meriwether Lewis*

Lewis's Woodpecker print by John James Audubon from *The Birds of America from Drawings made in the United States* (1842).

3. Nest cavities may be as low as 5 feet or as high as 100 feet.

4. Typical habitat

# Red-headed Woodpecker

**Description** Crimson head, black back, white underparts, white inner wing patches and rump

**Juveniles** Brownish head, brown-black back; may have some red on the head; may have barred wing patches

**Length** 9.25 inches

**Wingspan** 17 inches

**Range** Eastern United States, west through Great Plains

**Other Names** *Melanerpes erythrocephalus* (Scientific) white-shirt, half-a-shirt, shirt-tail bird, tricolored woodpecker
*Pic à tête rouge* (French)
*Carpintero de cabeza roja* (Spanish)

A favorite of many people due to its bright, glossy colors, crisp plumage pattern, and "extroverted" behavior of loud calls and activity out in the open.

## Identification
Medium-sized woodpecker with crimson red head, neck, throat, and upper breast; snow-white underparts and glossy black upperparts; thin black line between red head and white breast; large white wing patches; white rump and upper tail; tail black with white outer feathers.

Immatures might be confused with young sapsuckers, but Red-headeds have white patches on rear of wings and brown breast patch.

## Sounds
Call *kweeah*; weaker and less musical than Red-bellied.

Drum is short, weak, and slow.

## Habitat
Deciduous woodlands, prefers beech or oak; prefers dead or dying trees; also uses a wide variety of orchards, parks, farms, and savannas.

## Range
Breeds throughout the eastern United States west

1. Juveniles show little or no red on their heads.

# Better than Wood

Some woodpeckers have learned that drumming on metal signs, roofs, and downspouts can create an even louder sound than drumming on snags. And since the purpose of such drumming is to proclaim territory and attract a mate, the louder the better.

A Red-headed Woodpecker drums on a metal roof to proclaim its territory and attract a mate.

through the Great Plains; winters across southeastern third of the U.S.; winter abundance and location is related to availability of acorns or beech nuts.

Currently declining rapidly probably due to habitat loss, especially in the eastern United States; however, this species has fluctuated widely in abundance over the past two centuries, so it is hard to know precisely what is happening to it.

### Food

Most omnivorous of woodpeckers, eats insects, spiders, earthworms, nuts, bark, seeds, berries, fruit, small rodents, eggs and nestlings of other birds.

### Behavior Notes

Like Lewis's, Black-backed and American Three-toed Woodpeckers, Red-headed is a fire follower, opportunistically hunting and eating in burned over areas.

This is the most aggressive North American woodpecker species, willing to chase away a wide variety of other birds.

Caches (stores in hiding) food for winter consumption; breaks nuts to fit into cracks and crevices in posts or trees; stores nuts in railroad ties, under the shingles of houses, and under wet bark; observed catching grasshoppers and storing them alive by wedging them into cracks.

Frequently catches insects by fly-catching from a conspicuous perch (See sidebar next page).

Eggs are white; clutch size averages five to seven.

2. An agitated Red-headed fluffs its head feathers.

3. Open areas with scattered trees are preferred.

4. Acorns are one of the favored foods of this omnivorous woodpecker.

# Fly-catching

You may not think of woodpeckers "fly-catching" (flying out from a perch to catch flying insects in mid-air) much—after all, there is another entire group of birds named "flycatchers." It is an important technique for several species of woodpecker though. Lewis's Woodpeckers make impressive forays away from high perches to nab bugs, and Red-headed Woodpeckers also fly-catch.

5. Red-headed Woodpeckers have been known to nest in old telephone poles.

# Acorn Woodpecker

**Description** Medium-sized black-and-white woodpecker with a red crown, black back and mostly-black wings, with white on the face, white eyes, white rump, and white wing patches

**Juveniles** Similar in appearance to adult males, but with dark eyes, and without glossy shine on black feathers

**Length** 8.5 inches

**Wingspan** 17.5 inches

**Range** Western and southwestern United States, interior of Mexico, Central America

**Other Names** *Melanerpes formicivorus* (Scientific)
*Pic glandivore* (French)
*Carpintero de bellota* (Spanish; "acorn carpenter")

A corn Woodpeckers are sometimes described as "clown-like"—their bright eye against a dark back ground, mask-like facial colors, and squeaky calls do suggest the description.

## Identification

A stocky, medium-sized woodpecker; distinctive red cap, black facial area surrounding pale eyes, white forehead, throat can appear yellowish; black around base of bill; black back and wings with small white patches on wings and white rump; on the front of the head, males have only a white bar between the red cap and their bills; females have a black forehead bar between the cap and a white bar.

## Sounds

Typical two syllable *KETCH-up, KETCH-UP* repeated, but many sounds, chattering, noisy; a distinctive alarm call (two to three quick, harsh bursts) causes members of a colony to swing to the underside of a limb or freeze in place.

Drumming is two to 20 taps, slow, variable, sometimes accelerating.

## Habitat

Woods where oaks are present; may use mixed forests, even coniferous forests, but only when oaks are part of the mix; prefers woods where more than one oak species is present.

## Range

Year-round in western Oregon, the interior of California, much of Arizona, New Mexico, and far-western Texas; occurs in much of the interior of Mexico and Central America, ranging as far south as Columbia; throughout these areas, its

# Who is Woody?

Woody Woodpecker is a cartoon character created by Walter Lantz and produced from 1940 to 1972.

Judging by his field marks, Woody is clearly a woodpecker; but he is clearly not a member of a usual woodpecker species (for example, he is blue). His trademark call, "Ha-ha-ha-HAA-ha!" and the red crest could make one think he was patterned after a Pileated Woodpecker. However, ornithologist Kimball Garrett received a personal copy of Lantz's biography which states that Woody was inspired by Acorn Woodpeckers, which have a certain "clownish" appearance and can also make quite a racket with their calls.

Woody captures some of the characteristics that make us love woodpeckers— bright plumage, assertive activity, and surprising sounds.

range is defined by the rugged topography, and there are many parts of the range that are isolated from the broad area described above. It is often the most abundant woodpecker within its range.

### Food

Acorns up make up half the diet, which includes insects (especially flying ants), oak catkins (flowers), sap, and flower nectar; there are also records of Acorn Woodpeckers eating grass seeds, lizards, and bird eggs.

### Behavior Notes

Conspicuous when present, active and acrobatic;

Over a longer stretch, their flight undulates in typical woodpecker fashion, but less markedly so than many species.

In many areas, Cooper's Hawks are their most significant predator, although snakes may be a greater threat in some areas.

Acorn Woodpeckers often spend time in the canopies of trees, fly-catching from a high perch or plucking acorns from the tree or from granary holes. They rarely land on the ground, but may do so to pick up grit or dropped acorns. Unlike most woodpeckers, they don't often excavate to get at insects.

They will drill sap holes, but the holes are larger than sapsucker holes and not made in regular patterns on the trunk. They also will drink sap at sapsucker holes, and they will come to hummingbird feeders. Mostly a permanent resident, they may move in response to acorn crop failure.

The eggs are white and unmarked. Clutch size averages five eggs.

Breeding females do most incubating; breeding males do most of the nest-cleaning, and most adult members of the colony assist with feeding young.

1. Acorn Woodpecker using some acrobatics to get a good grasp on an acorn.

# Granaries

Acorn Woodpeckers store acorns in colonial "granary" trees filled with holes in the bark. The holes are plugged with acorns. Granary trees with more than 50,000 holes have been found. Colonies usually have one primary granary tree, but may add a nearby tree or two. Trees with thousands of holes indicate that acorn woodpeckers have used that tree for many generations, since any individual will not be able to make more than a few hundred holes in a year. The holes are made in winter in the outer bark, so they don't compromise the tree. Insect larvae sometimes live in the acorns and are eaten along with the acorn.

Acorn Woodpeckers are colonial, cooperative breeders, with complex interrelationships between individuals. Within any colony, one to seven males may breed with one to three females who lay their eggs in one nest cavity. Different sex configurations can hold within any one colony. Colonies include up to 15 individuals. One thought about the reason for the colonial nature of Acorn Woodpecker life is that the greater numbers help them defend their granaries against squirrels—an endless task.

Nest holes don't need to be in granary trees, but they will be nearby, in dead wood, 12 to 30 feet above ground. Acorn Woodpeckers excavate their own nest holes and they will usually make several other holes near the actual nest, for use as roosts or in case the main nest site fails.

# Gila Woodpecker

**Description** Heavily barred, black-and-white back and rump, central tail feathers also barred, other parts gray-brown, male has a red crown

**Juveniles** Similar to adults but with paler plumage and limited red on the head

**Length** 9.25 inches

**Wingspan** 16 inches

**Range** Southern Arizona, rare in southern California, range extends south through Baja California and the Pacific coast in Mexico

**Other Names** *Melanerpes uropygialis* (Scientific)
*Pic des saguaros* (French; "woodpecker of the Saguaros")
*Carpintero de Gila, Carpintero del desierto* (Spanish; "desert carpenter bird")

1

**G**ila Woodpecker is a noisy, assertive woodpecker of southwestern deserts. It is associated with open Saguaro deserts of southeastern Arizona, but its range extends beyond that of the Saguaro cactus. Its cavities are used by many other animal species.

### Identification

Medium-sized woodpecker with grayish tan head and underparts. The back, inner wing and tail are barred black and white. The belly is tinged with yellow and the forehead is white. The bill is black, and there are white wing patches. The male has a small red patch on the crown; otherwise, the sexes are similar.

Ladder-backed Woodpecker has black-and-white striped face and streaky underparts. Flickers are brown above with spotted underparts and different facial patterns. Note Gila's wing patches. Red-bellied and Golden-fronted do not overlap in range with Gila.

### Sounds

Loud, harsh *churr*, also loud laughing and squeaky sounds.

Drum long and steady.

### Habitat

Desert areas that have large enough trees or cacti for nest cavities; especially Saguaro desert, river bottoms and residential areas.

### Range

Southernmost Nevada, southeastern California, Arizona, south throughout Baja California and western Mexico.

# Smallest to Largest

The first number is the length; the second is the wingspan; all numbers are averages.

Downy Woodpecker 6.75" 12"
Ladder-backed Woodpecker 7.25" 13"
Nuttall's Woodpecker 7.25" 13"
Arizona Woodpecker 7.5" 14"
Am. Three-toed Woodpecker 8.25" 15"
Red-cockaded Woodpecker 8.5" 14"
Yellow-bellied Sapsucker 8.5" 16"
Red-breasted Sapsucker 8.5" 16"
Red-naped Sapsucker 8.5 16"
Acorn Woodpecker 8.5" 17.5"
Williamson's Sapsucker 9" 17"
Hairy Woodpecker 9.25" 15"
Gila Woodpecker 9.25" 16"
Red-bellied Woodpecker 9.25" 16"
White-headed Woodpecker 9.25" 16"
Red-headed Woodpecker 9.25" 17"
Golden-fronted Woodpecker 9.25" 17"
Black-backed Woodpecker 9.5" 15"
Lewis's Woodpecker 10.25" 21"
Gilded Flicker 11.5" 18"
Northern Flicker 12.5" 20"
Pileated Woodpecker 16.5" 29"

1. Female coming to a nest hole in a Saguaro cactus. Note that she lacks any red on the head.

### Food

Wide variety of insects, cactus fruit and pollen, nectar, seeds, small lizards, eggs, occasionally young of smaller birds.

### Behavior Notes

Gila Woodpeckers are noticeable residents of cities and suburbs. They are bold and noisy and will scavenge food from yards and visit hummingbird feeders. Usually does not excavate for food.

Frequently seen actively defending territory by chasing birds of many other species away by chasing and even attacking with its bill.

Nest 8 to 30 feet above ground in cactus, cottonwood, willow, large mesquite or palm.

Eggs pure white; clutch size three to five.

2. Sonoran Desert habitat with large Saguaro cactus suitable for nesting is ideal habitat.

# Saguaro Sympatry

**S**ympatry means living in the same place or having the same range. Saguaro is the name of the giant desert cacti (sometimes over 40 feet tall) in southern Arizona, California, and the state of Sonora, Mexico. Gila Woodpeckers, Gilded Flickers, White-winged Doves, Cactus Wrens, and a long hypothetical list of other species might use the same, individual cactus.

The Gila Woodpecker is an important species in the Sonoran Desert, where its cavities are used by many other animal species, including Lucy's Warbler, American Kestrel, Ferruginous Pygmy-Owl and Brown-crested Flycatcher.

A Gila excavates a nest cavity into the wet, soft interior a year before it will use it. The cactus responds by secreting a fluid that hardens into a scab to prevent water loss. These hardened holes sometimes survive beyond the life of the cactus and can be found on the ground near a decayed plant.

3

6

5

4

3. Gila Woodpecker returning to its nest cavity in a Saguaro.

4 & 5. Ferruginous Pygmy-Owl and Brown-crested Flycatcher nesting in old nest holes.

6. Even the pollen from the Saguaro flowers is eaten by the Gila.

# Golden-fronted Woodpecker

**Description** Black-and-white barred back, usually solid black rump, yellow-orange nape, male has red cap; golden wash on belly difficult to see

**Juveniles** Often with fine darker streaks on crown and breast; muted nape and nasal tuft color

**Length** 9.25 inches

**Wingspan** 17 inches

**Range** Throughout western Texas, south through most of eastern Mexico into Central America

**Other Names** *Melanerpes orifrons* (Scientific)
*Pic à front doré* (French)
*Carpintero cheje* (Spanish)

1

Stepping into the sweltering heat of July in Texas, I sat down on the porch in Roundtop, where we were staying, and heard an unfamiliar, loud, *churr* call repeated by a bird moving closer. A Golden-fronted Woodpecker jumped into view at the top of a telephone pole and made its contact call again, which was answered by another Golden-fronted that I could barely hear. They carried on about the business of finding food in spite of heat that slowed me to a standstill.

For many American birders, the widespread eastern species, Red-bellied Woodpecker, is the reference point for learning about Golden-fronteds, which are mainly found in Texas in the United States. That makes it seem as if Texas has its own kind of Red-bellied—flashier and bigger, just as you might expect!

### Identification

Medium-sized "zebra-striped" woodpecker with black-and-white barring across upperparts, but white rump and black tail with minimal barring on outer tail feathers. Yellow patch above the base of the bill, golden-yellow nape, red crown patch; rest of head, breast, and flanks grayish-tan; female lacks red crown patch.

Gila and Red-bellied have white wing patches and rump— Golden-fronted has black tail. Red-bellied has red crown (male) and nape; Gila has red crown patch (male).

### Sounds

Harsh, loud, level *cheer*; noticeably harsher than Red-bellied.

Drum is medium-speed, short.

# Woodpecker Flight

Golden-fronted Woodpeckers use what is considered the usual flight pattern for almost all woodpeckers—an undulating flight, with alternating, short periods of flapping and then tucking the wings to the body. Woodpeckers are heavy birds for their overall size, not known for soaring in the wind; bounding flight provides the most energy efficient pattern for them.

1. Male sports a red cap that the female lacks.

2

purple-stained face from eating Prickly Pear cactus fruit. Frequents orchards, pecan groves, suburbs and urban parks.

They will defend and use large territories, ranging farther than many other woodpeckers in search of food.

Permanent residents but will move for feeding sources.

Sometimes interbreeds with the Red-bellied Woodpecker.

Will excavate nest cavities in a variety of deciduous trees.

Eggs are white; clutch size averages four or five.

### Habitat
Prefers mesquite, river woodlands and orchards.

### Range
Southwestern Oklahoma, western and central Texas, south through eastern Mexico into Central America.

### Food
Easts mostly insects and other arthropods, but also acorns and other nuts, berries, fruits, seeds and corn.

### Behavior Notes
Does not excavate for food like many woodpeckers but forages for insects and fruit. Sometimes gets a

---

2. A Golden-fronted peeks out of its nest cavity near the Rio Grande River in Texas.

3

4

3 & 4. Golden-fronteds are not shy; here defending a perch from a Kiskadee (top) and a Green Jay (bottom).

# Frugivory

While no woodpeckers are strictly frugivores (fruit eaters), most species have been recorded eating fruit. In warmer climates or warmer weather, fruit at feeders will attract some woodpeckers. Bananas, grapes, apples, raisins, and halved cantaloupe and citrus fruits are all possibilities.

Golden-fronted Woodpecker eating a grapefruit at a feeding station. Pileated Woodpecker feasting on winter crabapples in a city park.

# Red-bellied Woodpecker

*Description* Black-and-white barring on back, buff underparts, male has red crown and nape, female has red nape, pink wash on belly difficult to see

*Juveniles* No red on the head, buff-colored bill

*Length* 9.25 inches

*Wingspan* 16 inches

*Range* Eastern United States west to Great Plains, breeding range extending northward in recent decades, uncommon visitor farther west and north

*Other Names* Melanerpes carolinus (Scientific) zebra woodpecker, Guinea sapsucker, orange sapsucker, cham-chack
*Pic à ventre rouge* (French)
*Carpintero de vientre rojo* (Spanish)

T his common eastern feeder bird has been moving its range northward for over 50 years. Like the Northern Cardinal, another southeastern bird now found throughout the north, Red-bellieds have probably benefited from forest fragmentation and the large increase in feeding stations, especially in recent decades.

## Identification

Medium-sized woodpecker with "zebra-striped" back. Males have a red forehead, crown, and nape; females have red only on the nape. The "red belly" is a pinkish wash on the lower belly; it is often hard to see (You can see this on the photo on the opposite page). The central tail feathers are barred white and black.

Throughout most of its range, its barred back is distinctive. Red-cockaded and Ladder-backed Woodpeckers have black facial marks and lack white wing patches and rump.

Similar Golden-fronted Woodpecker has yellow at the upper base of the bill and the entire nape is golden yellow. Golden-fronted's calls are harsher and deeper.

## Sounds

Loud *quirr*, that can sound surprisingly like a Wood Frog. Red-bellieds tend to move around fairly frequently when calling. If the sound moves, it's a bird not a frog, and if the sound remains stationary and you can't track down a bird visually, it's probably a frog. Also *chig-chig* and chuckling sounds.

Drumming is of medium speed and length, with steady tempo.

1. You can see the faint red wash on the belly of this bird that gives the species its common name.

# Superspecies

A superspecies is a group of species that is very closely related, though not interbreeding. There are four North American woodpecker superspecies:

Sapsuckers (not including Williamson's)

Gila/Red-bellied/Golden-fronted Woodpecker

Ladder-backed/Nuttall's Woodpecker

Northern/Gilded Flicker

If you are in an area where any two members of a superspecies are found, the nature of their interactions is always of interest to ornithologists.

Juvenile Red-bellied Woodpecker

# High Plains Drifters

A dozen or so pairs of bird species hybridize (successfully breed together) in the Great Plains, including one pair of sub-species and one pair of species of wood-peckers: Yellow-shafted and Red-shafted Flickers, and Red-bellied and Golden-fronted Woodpeckers.

In general, the Great Plains represent an enormous barrier to woodland species. At one time, it was thought that the introduction of European-style agriculture facilitated the hybridizing of these pairs, and it may have been a factor, but newer research suggests that the Great Plains hybrids were in existence even before the arrival of Europeans.

Much remains to be learned about how and why these pairs connected.

### Habitat
Can use a wide variety of habitats, but for breeding prefers forests with large enough trees for nest cavities and denser canopy than other woodpeckers.

### Range
Throughout the eastern United States, north to the northern-most tier of states and west to the Great Plains.

### Food
Two-thirds of diet is nuts (acorns, beech nuts, others), the rest is mostly insects, but also eats fruit and seeds.

### Behavior Notes
Rowing wingbeats, not bounding.

2

2. Red-bellieds can be found in eastern North America from the snow belt south to the palms of south Florida.

3

In cold climates, suet is the most attractive woodpecker food, but it is important to take it down when the weather gets above refrigerator temperature—warm suet can make the birds sick.

Many woodpeckers also like shelled peanuts. Unlike some other birds, woodpeckers cannot easily shell nuts and seeds—to do so, they have to haul the seed to a crevice and hammer it open, hoping they don't lose the prize inside in the process. Mealworms placed in a tray are readily eaten by many woodpeckers.

The structure of the feeder matters in feeding woodpeckers, which generally prefer being able to stay upright while they eat. If you want to attract larger woodpeckers, it is important to provide a large enough feeder to hold them.

Pair of Pileateds (male on left, female on right) share suet at a feeding station.

3. A good look at the zebra-striped back pattern. Golden-fronteds also show this but lack the red head.

# Williamson's Sapsucker

**Description**  Male has black back, white rump, large white wing patches, black head with two white stripes, red throat, black breast, yellow belly; female overall brown, some yellow on belly, no white wing patches, no red

**Juveniles**  Resemble adult of their sex, males have white throat

**Length**  9 inches

**Wingspan**  17 inches

**Range**  Mountains of western U.S., south into Mexico

**Other Names**  *Sphyrapicus thyroideus* (Scientific)
*Pic de Williamson* (French)
*Chupasavia de Williamson, Carpintero garganta roja* (Spanish; "red-throated carpenter bird")

Williamson's Sapsuckers are often quiet and inconspicuous. They can be hard to locate, but both sexes—as different in appearance as they are—are striking and winsome in the muted light of the deep forest.

This species was named for Robert Stockton Williamson (1824–1882), who surveyed rail routes in the west in the 1850s. Perhaps it should have been named "Newberry's Sapsucker," since John Newberry was the scientist who collected the first specimen (on one of Williamson's expeditions). Newberry was also the first geologist to visit the Grand Canyon.

### Identification

Medium-sized woodpecker; male has white wing patches, rump, eyeline, and mustache stripe, iridescent black upperparts and breast, red patch on chin and upper throat, yellow belly; female has brown head; upperparts, wings and flanks barred with white, brown and black; black breast, yellow belly and white rump.

Male is unmistakable in its range; female may be confused with other sapsuckers, but has brown head with no red and no white wing patches.

Females may resemble flickers but have unspotted bellies and browner, less-patterned heads. Female Williamson's have brown heads, dark brown-and-white barring on backs, wings, and sides, and dark breast patches with some yellow on the belly, but no white wing patches or red markings.

### Sounds

Clear *kweeah* call; less mewing than other sapsuckers.

# Vive la Différence!

The male and female Williamson's Sapsuckers look so different that early naturalists thought they were two different species. It wasn't until 1873 that Henry Henshaw verified that they are of the same species when he found a mated pair nesting in Colorado.

Female Williamson's look so different than the male that they were considered separate species for many years.

1. Note the male's beak full of ants—a favorite meal of Williamson's.

Drum begins with fast outburst followed by taps with longish pauses.

### Habitat
Mid- to high-elevation coniferous forests and mixed coniferous forests.

### Range
Appropriate mountainous habitat in Pacific Northwest, Rocky Mountains, Great Basin, Sierras, winters south into Mexico.

### Food
Sap and tree matter prior to breeding season, then mostly ants during the breeding season; more dependent on ants than any other North American woodpecker.

### Behavior Notes
Williamson's are generally quiet and can be hard to find. They will sometimes share the same deciduous woods used by a Red-breasted or Red-naped Sapsucker.

Thought to migrate along mountain ridges to the south in fall, with most spending the winter at fairly high elevations.

Eggs white; average clutch size five or six.

2. Dry western forest dominated by Ponderosa Pine is a favorite habitat of the Williamson's Sapsucker.

# Sap & Ants

Like the other sapsuckers, Williamson's drills sap wells in regular patterns on tree trunks and then use the wells to drink sap and catch insects attracted to the sap. But sap is a valuable commodity and while the sapsuckers are absent, squirrels, mice and hummingbirds may stop by for a sweet snack. Over thirty species of birds have been noted to feed on tree sap.

3

3. Making the rounds; a male Williamson's checks on his sap wells.

Sapsucker sap wells in a young pine in Grand Teton National Park.

# Yellow-bellied Sapsucker

**Description** Distinctive woodpecker with red forehead, crown and throat, black and yellow bib and mottled back

**Juveniles** Mottled with white mustache and eyebrows; same white rump and wing patches as adults

**Length** 8.5 inches

**Wingspan** 16 inches

**Range** Alaska across Canada, extending south into the northeastern U.S.; migrates south in fall

**Other Names** *Sphyrapicus varius* (Scientific) squealer
*Pic maculé* (French)
*Carpintero de paso, Chupasavia maculado, Chupasavia vientreamarillo* (Spanish; "yellow-bellied sapsucker")

1

Every spring a Yellow-bellied Sapsucker stops at the maple tree in our front yard for a few days, visiting rows of holes made in past years that fill with sap in the spring, and probably adding some new ones.

Those regular rows of small holes are a sure sign that at some point, one of the sapsuckers has been visiting a tree.

This species was lumped with Red-naped and Red-breasted Sapsuckers until 1983. The species hybridize at the margins of their ranges.

### Identification

Small woodpecker with black bib on breast, red forehead and crown, black on the back of the head, black stripe on the side of the head bordered by two white stripes, white rump and wing patches, black back with yellow barring, underparts tinged with yellow; chin and throat red in male; white in female.

Closest in appearance to Red-naped Sapsucker, but Yellow-bellied has a white nape, and the red throat is bordered by a broad, black bar.

Immature sapsuckers are among the "foolers" in bird identification, suggesting

1. Male attending its drilled sap wells.   2. Female drinking "pseudo sap," (sugar water) from hummingbird feeder.

# Damage Control

It can be hard to keep woodpeckers from sampling the bugs in your beautiful wood siding or shingles, but here are a few ideas:

1) Get the bugs out of the wood. Woodpeckers are usually drawn to your wood by food. Can you remove the source?

2) What's inside? Woodpeckers may be attracted to your structure by the sound inside. Check for clocks, dehumidifiers, radios, televisions (or anything that might sound vaguely like insects) inside the area where the woodpeckers are drilling. Moving the sound might remove the attraction.

3) Make it inconvenient. Anything that you can hang over the area, especially if it can blow in the breeze, might be a deterrent.

4) Cover it up. Netting or some other covering will stop the drilling, but it might be expensive and inconvenient.

5) You can try visual (plastic owls, etc.) or noisy (falcon calls, etc.) deterrents, but they may not work to begin with, and after a while, the offending birds tend to become acclimated. If you see a woodpecker yawning near your owl, you'll know it didn't work.

several other species: Immature Red-headed Woodpecker is similar but is dull white with dark streaks below. Female Williamson's Sapsucker is similar but lacks white on the face and is sharply barred on the back and sides.

Juvenile sapsuckers have barred black-and-white backs and lack bright colors, so they might be confused with American Three-toed Woodpeckers; given an adequate look, however, the rest of the plumage is quite different.

### Sounds

Similar for all three sapsucker species: wide array of sounds, but frequent sounds include nasal *kweeah* or cat-like *mew*; *wika-wika-wika* series.

Drumming is irregular, often with an opening burst followed by slowing and syncopated taps; sometimes described as "morse-code." They will drum on metal signs and other man-made items that resonate loudly (See sidebar on pg. 7).

### Habitat

Prefers young forests, presumably due to relative ease of obtaining sap, often found in open, logged-over woodland with some remaining birch or aspen; frequently chooses nest sites near water.

### Range

Breeds from Alaska across most of Canada, with range extending south into a broad band of the northeastern United States as far west as Minnesota; winters across the southeastern U.S. and throughout eastern Mexico and Central America.

### Food

They specialize in sipping sap and eating insects attracted to the sap (See sidebar next page).

### Behavior Notes

Sapsuckers seem to be in no hurry to get away, going about their drilling-for-sap work in a desultory but persistent way. Nevertheless, they will attempt to defend areas of sap wells from other species, such as Ruby-throated Hummingbirds, that try to get at the sap.

Prefers dead trees for nests; the trees must be large enough to contain a nest cavity; pairs are monogamous; male does most excavating; both sexes participate in incubation and feeding young.

Eggs are white; the average clutch size is four or five eggs.

3. Mom returns to the nest with a beak full of insects for the hungry and noisy nestlings.

# Sucking Sap

Sapsuckers are the only woodpeckers that excavate specifically to get at sap, but other species will occasionally also drink sap if the opportunity presents itself. Sapsuckers are specialized for sipping tree sap; their tongues are shorter and less extensible than those of other woodpeckers, tipped with stiff hairs to collect sap. Some insects and other arthropods may be trapped in sap or captured at sap wells; this prey is a key food during the breeding season, although sap is always a part of the diet. They also eat small amounts of tree material excavated from sap wells; also fruits and seeds.

Female stripping bark to allow sap to ooze out (left); Rows of sap wells drilled into a Paper Birch (middle); Sapsucker eyeing a wasp that was no doubt attracted to the same sap the sapsucker was interested in (right).

# Red-naped Sapsucker

**Description** Similar to Yellow-bellied Sapsucker; all-red throat with black border, black bib, red forehead, black stripe along the side of the head bordered by two white stripes; female usually has white chin with some red; both sexes have red nape; rump white; large white wing patches

**Juveniles** Nestlings mottled with black and white, white mustache and eyebrows

**Length** 8.5 inches

**Wingspan** 16 inches

**Range** Southern British Columbia and western U.S.

**Other Names** *Sphyrapicus nuchalis* (Scientific)
*Pic à nuque rouge* (French)
*Chupasavia nuquirroja* (Spanish; "red-naped sapsucker")

R ed-naped Sapsucker is the typical sapsucker of the wooded interior of the western United States. It spends more time in deciduous forests than the farther-west Red-breasted Sapsucker, but frequents a wide range of mixed forests.

This species was lumped with Yellow-bellied and Red-breasted Sapsuckers until 1983. The species hybridize at the margins of their ranges.

### Identification

Can be confused with Yellow-bellied Sapsucker. The male Red-naped Sapsucker has little to no black border around the red chin. The back of a Red-naped shows less white than Yellow-bellied, arrayed in longitudinal stripes that extend down each side of the back.

### Sounds

Sounds: similar for all three sapsucker species: nasal *kweeah* or cat-like *mew*; *wika-wika-wika* series.

Drumming is an opening burst followed by slowing and syncopated taps; sometimes described as "morse-code."

### Habitat

Deciduous or mixed forests, usually including aspen.

### Range

Breeds from British Columbia south through the Rocky Mountains to Arizona; winters in Mexico, Arizona and New Mexico.

# Identifying Hybrids

In or near areas where more than one species are known to occur, particular care should be taken in identifying individual birds to species. Learn the primary characteristics of the "pure" individuals, and try to find any differing features of individuals you see in the field. It may not be possible to safely identify every individual, but the effort to check each one carefully will be rewarding.

Red-naped with wasp that it likely caught at one of its sap wells.

# Red-breasted Sapsucker

*Description*  Sapsucker with red head, neck and breast; except for hybrid birds, it is not likely that this species will be confused with other species.

*Juveniles*  Red-breasted fledglings have a black crown and a brown wash over the red on the head and breast; head and breast darker than other sapsucker species

*Length*  8.5 inches

*Wingspan*  16 inches

*Range*  West coast of Canada and the United States

*Other Names*  *Sphyrapicus ruber* (Scientific)
*Pic à poitrine rouge* (French)
*Chupasavia pechirroja* (Spanish)

R ed-breasted Sapsucker is the typical sapsucker of the humid woodlands of the Pacific Northwest. This species was lumped with Yellow-bellied and Red-naped Sapsuckers until 1983.

### Identification

Small woodpecker; entire head red except for black spot in front of eyes and white line just above the bill; red on head extends to nape and breast; large white wing-patch, back black with variable white or yellow spots, belly yellow; sexes alike.

### Sounds

Similar for all three sapsucker species: nasal *kweeah* or cat-like *mew*; *wika-wika-wika* series.

Drumming is similar to other sapsuckers; Morse-code-like.

### Habitat

Prefers coniferous forests but will sometimes use mixed forests along rivers and the coast.

### Range

Breeds from southeastern Alaska south as far as northern California and the Sierras; winters all along the United States coast south just across the Mexican border.

### Food

Drinks from sap wells all year long.

### Behavior Notes

A short-distance migrant that moves in small groups, sometimes with Williamson's Sapsuckers.

Rufous Hummingbirds will follow Red-breasteds around and feed at their sap wells.

## Ant Truffles

Sapsuckers of all three species eat ants and other arthropods (animals with no back-bone, but having a segmented body and legs). When catching ants to feed their nestlings, they sometimes take the ant to one of their sap wells and dip it in sap. Presumably this adds some nutritional value, but who knows, maybe they need to disguise the ant to get the kids to eat it!

# Ladder-backed Woodpecker

**Description**  Black-and-white barred back, buff underparts with black flecks, face buff-colored with narrow black frame, male has extensive red crown, female has black crown

**Juveniles**  Dingier in appearance than adults; both sexes may have small red caps

**Length**  7.25 inches

**Wingspan**  13 inches

**Range**  Southwest from Colorado and Texas

**Other Names**  *Picoides scalaris* (Scientific)
cactus woodpecker
*Pic arlequin* (French)
*Carpintero chilillo, Carpintero mexicano,
Carpintero listado* (Spanish; "striped carpenter bird")

D ue to their ability to thrive without large-diameter trees, Ladder-backed Woodpeckers may pop up anywhere within their southwestern range.

This woodpecker is closely related to Nuttall's; they may interbreed where their ranges meet in southeastern California.

## Identification

Small black-and-white woodpecker with barred upperparts; the underparts are light buff color with spots and streaks on sides, flanks, and undertail. The tail is black, but barred with white on the three outermost feathers. The head is red toward the back, spotted on the crown, and black-and-white with red spots on the forehead (black spots for female).

Gila Woodpecker has white patches on wings and rump and no facial stripes. Barred back distinguishes Ladder-backed from Downy, Hairy and Arizona Woodpeckers. Nuttall's has more crisp overall appearance with black bars on back noticeably wider than white bars.

## Sounds

Sharp *pik*, lower than Downy Woodpecker, rattle ends with grating tones.

Drum is a rapid buzz, shorter and faster than Nuttall's Woodpecker.

## Habitat

Found in deserts and scrubby, dry habitat, as well as open pine forests.

# Stiff Tails

Ladder-backed Woodpeckers (and every woodpecker species) have stiff, strong tail feathers that allow them to brace their bodies against tree trunks to stabilize themselves as they drill, hammer and feed.

1 & 2. Stiff tail feathers help while feeding on Ocotillo flowers (top) and dried Cholla cactus stem.

### Range

Southeastern Colorado, south through western Texas, much of New Mexico and Arizona, southern tip of Nevada, southeastern California, almost all of Mexico.

### Food

Mostly insects and other arthropods.

### Behavior Notes

Forages for bugs among cactus and mesquite. Because of their small size, Ladder-backs can use small patches of brush and trees; the other desert woodpeckers, Gila Woodpecker and Gilded Flicker, need larger-sized cacti or trees for their nests, so they do not compete with Ladder-backed for these smaller pockets of brush.

Ladder-backed Woodpeckers optimize their foraging by sexual specialization: females hunt higher in trees, males focus on lower trunks and branches.

3. Adult female feeding a recently fledged male.

4. Females lack any red on head.

## Mi Casa, Su Casa

The lives of Ladder-backed Woodpeckers are good examples of how important woodpeckers can be in ecosystems. Ash-throated Flycatchers and Elf Owls live throughout the range of Ladder-backed Woodpeckers, and though both are cavity nesters, neither can make their own cavities. Both utilize nest boxes, but also rely on Ladder-backed Woodpeckers to make the cavities that they need for their nests.

5 & 6. Elf Owl and Ash-throated Flycatcher nesting in abandoned Ladder-backed Woodpecker cavities in Agave stalks (Big Bend, TX).

# Nuttall's Woodpecker

**Description** Small black-and-white woodpecker

**Juveniles** Similar to adults but with buffy under-parts, whiter upperparts, and both sexes show red in crown

**Length** 7.25 inches

**Wingspan** 13 inches

**Range** Throughout California in appropriate habi-tat, rare in southern Nevada, range extends just south of the border into Mexico

**Other Names** *Picoides nuttallii* (Scientific)
*Pic de nuttall* (French)
*Carpintero de nuttall, Carpintero californiano* (Spanish; "California carpenter bird")

1

Nuttall's is a small, acrobatic woodpecker whose range is almost entirely within the state of California. I first saw them in a city park, and even in that relatively brief encounter, those two birds were all over the oak tree they were in—on the ground, on the trunk, in the crown, and even foraging along small branches.

## Identification

Small black-and-white woodpecker; upperparts are black with white barring; underparts are white with some barring on sides, flanks and undertail; sexes are alike, except that the male has red on the back of the head.

Downy and Hairy Woodpeckers not barred on back.

On average, slightly larger than Ladder-backed Woodpecker; best distinguished by vocalizations, by narrower white stripes on face and by back pattern—solid black area on upper back and narrow white strips and wider black stripes.

Immature Yellow-bellied Sapsucker has mottled, not barred back, mottled underparts and white wing patches.

Thought to hybridize with Downy and Ladder-backed. At edges of range, individuals should be examined carefully for signs of hybridization.

## Sounds

Sharp, rising two-part *petek*; level, steady rattle call.

Drum is steady, medium speed, long; longer and faster than Downy.

1. Male Nuttall's has red on the head; females lack this mark.

# Name Game

Woodpecker names are among the most amusing of the many funny bird names in English. Who didn't snicker or at least lift an eyebrow the first time they heard, "Yellow-bellied Sapsucker"?

The two "three-toed" species have had their English names changed repeatedly as the research of the day has shifted them around the taxonomic landscape. One or the other has sometimes been Arctic Three-toed Woodpecker, or Northern Three-toed Woodpecker or Black-backed Three-toed Woodpecker.

Northern Flicker (once upon a time split into Yellow-shafted and Red-shafted Flicker) is a catchy name that reflects the difference between this species and the other woodpeckers, although it does confuse people occasionally.

For Pileated Woodpecker, the issue is how to say the name: PILL-ee-ate-ed or PILE-ee-ate-ed, or even PILE-ate-ed. I have heard PILL-ee-ate-ed much more than the others, but I do still hear the other variations on occasion.

There are some great names among the over 200 species of woodpeckers found around the world: Eurasian Wryneck, Ocellated Piculet, Melancholy Woodpecker, Fernandina's Flicker, Powerful Woodpecker, and Robust Woodpecker—not to mention Hairy Woodpecker as a name for an animal with feathers!

## Habitat

Prefers oak woodland in the northern part of its range but uses a greater variety of trees in the south.

## Range

Almost entirely in California, extending just into southern Nevada and northern Baja California; found throughout California in appropriate habitat.

## Food

Mostly insects and other arthropods; heavily associated with oaks, but doesn't eat many acorns.

## Behavior Notes

Forages in uncharacteristic (for woodpeckers in general) manner of creeping and hopping.

Eggs are white; clutch size averages four to five.

2. Male Nuttall's showing off its acrobatic abilities.

# The First Field Guide

**N**uttall's Woodpecker is named after Thomas Nuttall (1786-1859), a self-taught English naturalist. His book about birds, *A Manual of the Ornithology of the United States and Canada*, written in 1832 and illustrated with woodcuts, stayed in print into the twentieth century. It was the first book that could be called a field guide.

Thomas Nuttall (1786-1859)

FLICKER, or GOLDEN-WINGED WOODPECKER.

(*Picus auratus*, L. Wilson, i. p. 45. pl. 3. fig. 1. [male]. Audubon, pl. 37. Orn. Biog. i. p. 191. Phil. Museum, No.  )

Sp. Charact. — Umber-brown, barred with black ; beneath yellowish-white, spotted with black : a black crescent on the breast ; a crimson red crescent on the hind head ; wings and tail beneath, and shafts of all the larger feathers, golden-yellow. — The *male* alone with black mustachios. — *Young*, dull grey, without either the red or black crescent.

This beautiful and well known bird breeds and inhabits throughout North America, from Labrador to Florida, being partially migratory only from Canada and the Northern States, proceeding to the south in October, and returning north in April. It has also been observed on

# Downy Woodpecker

*Description* Smallest North American woodpecker; black and white plumage with broad white stripe down back, usually dark spots on outer tail feathers, male has a red spot near the back of the head

*Juveniles* Similar to adults but juvenile male has red on the forehead and no red patch on the nape

*Length* 6.75 inches

*Wingspan* 12 inches

*Range* Across the U.S. and Canada, found in every state and all the Canadian provinces

*Other Names* *Picoides pubescens* (Scientific)
little sapsucker, willow woodpecker
*Pic mineur* (French)
*Pájaro carpintero peludo* (Spanish; "furry carpenter bird")

Downy Woodpecker is one of the most widespread of all bird species in North America. Many live in forests, but they are also one of the handful of species that show up in almost everyone's backyard.

The counterintuitive bird name, Downy Woodpecker, was given to this species by Swedish biologist Carl von Linné (Carolus Linnaeus), who came up with our taxonomic system in the eighteenth century. Linneaus never saw a Downy Woodpecker, but using the American Mark Catesby's description of the white back feathers as "downy" as opposed to the similar, but much stiffer feathers of the species that came to be known as "hairy."

(Linneaus did see a small woodpecker, *Dendrocopos minor*—in Swedish, *Mindre Hackspett*, or "smaller woodpecker" that lives like a Downy Woodpecker, but isn't closely related.)

## Identification

Small, black-and-white woodpecker; white on center of back; underparts are unmarked and vary geographically—usually white, but grayish-white in the west; sexes are alike except for a red patch on the nape of the male.

Downy Woodpeckers are most easily confused with Hairy Woodpeckers, which are larger. Without direct size comparison, the easiest way to separate them is to look at the size of the bill in relation to the head. Downy Woodpeckers have small, stubby bills that appear to be roughly half the length as the depth of the head. Hairy Woodpeckers have robust bills that are roughly the same length as the depth of their heads.

# Drumming

Woodpeckers make rapid, rolling, drumming sounds. These drums are usually used either to alert potential mates, defend territory or to maintain contact between members of existing family groups.

Sometimes species can be identified by their drumming patterns (details in species accounts), but it takes a practiced ear to know for sure and most drumming cannot be identified without other evidence of the species.

Small birds of other species may be attracted to drumming woodpeckers, presumably because the presence of a woodpecker might mean the presence of tasty insects!

2

1. Male Downy showing his red nape. Female lacks this.

2. Females do not show any red.

Other differences which are harder to see, include the Downy's barred outer tail feathers (Hairy has white outer tail feathers), and Downy's red nape patch, which is never divided in two (Hairy's is often divided).

Downys are often found on small plants, even stiff grass and weeds. Hairy forages almost exclusively on trees. Downy Woodpeckers are also more "tame" and less likely to flee in human presence.

## Sounds

Bright *pik* call, silvery, cascading "laugh" or "whinny."

Drum is slow and short with brief pauses, strokes often separable.

## Habitat

Common throughout its range in open, deciduous woodlands, but also found in coniferous forests if there are some deciduous plants in the understory.

## Range

Across northern North America, found in every state and all the Canadian provinces.

## Food

Insects and other arthropods, fruits, seeds, sap and some tree tissue.

## Behavior Notes

Downy Woodpeckers optimize finding food by dividing foraging methods by sex: males peck, females probe. In addition, each sex spends more time on particular tree species.

Does not migrate; large counts of these woodpeckers (sometimes in the hundreds) moving past migration nodes are likely dispersing birds taking advantage of the same conditions that cause migrants to concentrate.

Like many birds, Downy Woodpeckers will take

3. Side-by-side size comparison of a Downy (left) and a Hairy Woodpecker (right).

water baths or dust baths to deter parasites, but Downys have also been observed taking snow baths and sunbathing by spreading their feathers out along a horizontal branch.

As part of courtship, male and female will follow each other through the woods, holding their wings high and then flapping them slowly in a manner that has been described as butterfly-like or bat-like, making long loops through the forest.

Eggs are glossy and white; clutch size is four to eight. The male incubates the eggs at night, and sexes take turns during the day.

Except during nesting, each individual roosts in its own cavity at night, and Downy Woodpeckers may frequently make new cavities for this purpose. They have been observed making cavities during every month of the year.

This is a very common woodpecker. Christmas Bird Counts on the East Coast indicate that there may be three times as many Downy Woodpeckers there as the next most common woodpecker, Northern Flicker. A couple of band-ing studies at bird feeders showed that numerous individuals were using the feeders, but not all at once, so observers may have thought there were fewer birds. One researcher banded 21 birds over a two-year peri-od; the other banded 88 in less than a year.

4

These tiny square holes in Paper Birch look like the result of a well-ordered design, but they are squared off because of the horizontal peeling nature of birch bark, not the intent of the woodpecker. Downys make a vertical cut then peel back the bark in search of a soft scale insect (family Coccidae: *Xylococcus betulae*) that winters just below the outer bark. Sometimes they leave a hinge (and hence a door-like flap, and sometimes they cut both sides and the resulting hole is more window-like (as in this photo).

4. A Downy has broken into this goldenrod gall to get at the larvae inside.

# Hairy Woodpecker

**Description** Medium-sized black-and-white woodpecker with robust bill and broad white strip on back, tail feathers usually clear white, male has red spot on the back of the head

**Juveniles** Young are streaked or barred on underparts; male may have yellow-orange or red in the crown; female may have red in the crown

**Length** 9.25 inches

**Wingspan** 15 inches

**Range** Across most of Canada, the U.S. and Mexico

**Other Names** *Picoides villosus* (Scientific)
big sapsucker
*Pic chevelu* (French)
*Carpintero-velloso mayor* (Spanish)

This is another common woodpecker, often found in close contact with Downy Woodpeckers. Hairy Woodpeckers are often noisier than Downys, but they tend to be more solitary and far less tame.

## Identification

Medium-sized with plumage that varies widely across its broad range. Largest birds are in the north. Most birds have white underparts, black upperparts with a white stripe down the center of the back, black wings with white spots, and a black tail with white outer tail feathers. The sexes are alike, except the male has a red band on the back of the head, often into two spots in eastern birds.

All Hairy Woodpeckers have proportionally long, robust bills for their size.

Hairy Woodpeckers are most easily confused with Downy Woodpeckers, which are smaller. Without direct size comparison, the easiest way to separate them is to look at the size of the bill in relation to the head. Downy Woodpeckers have small, stubby bills that appear to be roughly half the length as the depth of the head. Hairy Woodpeckers have robust bills that are roughly the same length as the depth of their heads. The calls and sounds of Hairy Woodpeckers are lower in pitch and more forceful than those of Downy Woodpeckers.

Hairys are also distinguished from other similar woodpeckers in most places by their unmarked, white outer tail feathers.

## Birds of Different Feathers

In winter, Downy Woodpeckers often move through the woods in flocks that include several other species: Black-capped Chickadee, Tufted Titmouse, Red-breasted Nuthatch, White-breasted Nuthatch, and possibly others.

Sticking together in a tough time of year provides several advantages: more eyes means mean a better chance of detecting predators before they can strike, and the birds can work together to find scarce food.

Other woodpecker species also join mixed flocks from time-to-time for the same reasons.

1. Males show a red mark on the back of the head. Females lack this spot of color.

## Sounds

Makes a loud, distinct *peek* call; and a long rattle call that is quite different from Downy—lower pitched and more grating.

Drumming is fast, with strokes often inseparable, and long pauses between rolls.

## Habitat

A wide range of forest types; prefers larger trees than Downy.

## Range

From the treeline south across Alaska, all of Canada, and all of the United States in appropriate habitat, range extends south through Mexico into Central America.

## Food

About three quarters of its diet is insects and other arthropods, but also eats a wide variety of fruits and seeds.

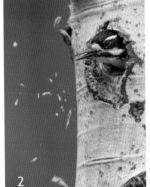

## Behavior Notes

Hairy Woodpeckers are energetic and often fairly conspicuous as they flake and excavate tree trunks in search of food.

The plumage on their back, white along the top, then dark, then pied black and white spots on the flanks, is ideal for providing camouflage in the forest.

2. Enthusiastic excavation; a male Hairy creates a nest cavity in an aspen with heart rot.

3. Male bringing a juicy beetle grub back to the nest hole.

# Eastern, Intermountain & Pacific Hairy Woodpeckers

**B**irds in the western part of the range may have less white on the upperparts and consequently appear much darker. "Pacific" Hairys typically have buffy or gray underparts rather than white. A few remote populations do have some black in the outer tail feathers (in Newfoundland and the Bahamas, for example). Intermountain Hairy has fewer white spots on the wings than the Eastern Hairy and a darker back. The Eastern Hairy shows much more white on the head and back than the western forms.

Hairy Woodpeckers on the Pacific coast (right) are darker than eastern birds (left) and intermountain form (center)

# Arizona Woodpecker

**Description** Small woodpecker of southeastern Arizona with a distinctive solid brown back; male has red on head that female lacks

**Juveniles** Similar to adults, but with more muted colors and less-extensive red

**Length** 7.5 inches

**Wingspan** 14 inches

**Range** Southeastern Arizona; range extends well south into Mexico

**Other Names** *Picoides arizonae* (Scientific)
Strickland's woodpecker, brown-backed woodpecker
*Pic d'Arizona* (French)
*Carpintero de Arizona* (Spanish)

O ne of around three dozen bird species that live mostly in Mexico but whose ranges extend north across the border in Arizona or New Mexico.

### Identification

Dark, muted, brown-backed with a brown eye stripe. Heavily spotted with brown below; tail brown with white barred outer feathers; rump brown; wings barred; solid brown back, rump, wing coverts are distinctive. Male has red on head; female does not. Other brown-backed woodpeckers have some barring and white rumps.

### Sounds

Sharp, high *peek*, like a hoarse Hairy Woodpecker; also a descending, rattle call. Drum is long with three per minute.

### Habitat

Oak forest in canyons and mountains; usually found at lower elevations than Hairy Woodpecker and higher elevations than Ladder-backed Woodpecker.

### Range

Mountains of SE Arizona and extreme SW New Mexico.

### Food

Mostly insects, especially beetles; some berries, fruits, acorns.

### Behavior Notes

Does not migrate, but may change elevations in winter according to food supply.

Becomes exceptionally quiet and secretive during breeding season. Both sexes excavate and incubate. Eggs white; average clutch size two to four.

---

1. Note the Arizona's solid brown back. No other North American woodpecker has this field mark.

# The Woodpecker formerly known as Strickland's

This species and a closely-related group of woodpeckers in Central Mexico were known until about 15 years ago as Strickland's Woodpecker; books published before that time will use that name. The American Ornithologists' Union decided at that time that the two were distinct enough to be separated, so the mostly American bird became Arizona Woodpecker, and the mostly Mexican species remains Strickland's Woodpecker (*Picoides stricklandi*).

Often works bark while holding body at an angle, not vertically. May even hang upside down while working. Often flies to the bottom of a tree trunk and then works its way up in a spiral.

# Red-cockaded Woodpecker

**Description**  Black-and-white barred back, black cap, large white cheek patch; red "cockade" of feathers behind the eye of males difficult to see

**Juveniles**  Similar to adults but brownish; may have red on center of crown or forehead

**Length**  8.5 inches

**Wingspan**  14 inches

**Range**  Southeastern United States in appropriate habitat, declining across range

**Other Names**  *Picoides borealis* (Scientific)
*Pic à face blanche* (French; "white-faced woodpecker")
*Carpintero cara blanco* (Spanish; "white-faced carpenter bird")

1

The nesting habits of Red-cockaded Woodpeckers are a marked difference between this species and the others described in this book. Red-cockadeds prefer live trees for their cavities, and due to the hardness of the live sapwood and copious sap flow of live trees, these cavities may take up to twelve years to complete. That means some cavities are begun in the lifetime of one woodpecker and finished by another.

It also means that Red-cockaded Woodpeckers are tenaciously attached to their nesting areas and may stay in one place even as the habitat around them is changed into a less hospitable environment (by being logged, for example); and it also means that once you find a nesting area, you may be able to find the woodpeckers there for a number of years.

### Identification

Medium-sized black-and-white woodpecker with a barred back and large white patches on the sides of the head. These patches are an easy way to separate this bird from all others in its range. Red-cockadeds also have heavy dark spots on the sides and flanks. Male has a tiny red strip ("cockade") on each side of the head above the white patch—this is difficult to see in the wild.

### Sounds

Long, nasal *skwiit* call; more likely to be confused with a Brown-headed Nuthatch or a European Starling than another woodpecker.

Drum is infrequent and quiet.

# An Endangered Species

Red-cockaded Woodpecker is listed under the United States Endangered Species Act of 1973, which means that the existence of the species is considered threatened by human activity. In the case of the Red-cockaded Woodpecker, the main threat is loss of habitat (see page 59).

Unlike most woodpeckers, Red-cockadeds excavate cavities in live trees with no heart rot.

1. Note the tiny patch of red feathers on this male. That is the "cockade."

### Habitat

Prefers open mature pine forest kept open by forest fires at least every five years; known to use Longleaf, Loblolly, Slash, Shortleaf, Virginia, Pond, and Pitch Pines. They may be surprisingly persistent in staying at a nest site, probably due to the difficulty of making cavities in living wood and the longevity of these cavities. Sometimes birds will not abandon a nesting area even if all of the surrounding area has been clearcut. Eventually, however, they need to leave such an area.

### Range

Southeastern United States north to Virginia and Kentucky, west to East Texas and Oklahoma; uncommon throughout.

### Food

Arthropods found on or near pine trees, especially ants, but also beetles, fruit, and seeds.

### Behavior Notes

Red-cockaded Woodpeckers optimize their foraging by sexual specialization: females forage low on tree trunks, males forage high in the canopy.

Unlike most other woodpeckers, Red-cockaded Woodpecker excavates its holes in live trees (one of several species of pine); these holes may then be used for decades. Another interesting feature of the nest hole is that bark is scraped away around the nest entrance, producing resin flow and buildup. It is thought that the resins protect the nest from Rat Snakes.

Red-cockaded Woodpeckers make multiple cavities in a nesting area, but only use one for the nest. These extra cavities may be used if the first one fails, they can provide roosting or escape holes, and they present a puzzle to predators.

Red-cockadeds are monogamous but raise their young in a colony with the help of nonbreeding males (less than five percent of "helpers" are females).

# Rare Habitat

Red-cockaded Woodpeckers have particular narrow requirements for their breeding territories: mature open pine forest that burns frequently during the summer (every one to five years). As the Southeast has become more settled in recent centuries, both extensive pine forests and natural forest fires have become rarer. This has been hard on the Red-cockaded Woodpecker, which has declined through the last century.

Colored leg bands help researchers keep track of breeding birds (left). Nestling male peeks out from cavity surrounded by oozing pitch (middle). Longleaf Pine nest trees; some with several cavities (note the painted white bands that mark the trees).

# White-headed Woodpecker

*Description* White head and throat, white wing patches, body black, male has a red patch on the back of the head

*Juveniles* Duller, browner black; wing patch is barred or spotted; both sexes show red in the crown

*Length* 9.25 inches

*Wingspan* 16 inches

*Range* Mountain forests of Washington, Oregon and California; uncommon visitor to nearby areas of lower elevation, especially in winter

*Other Names* *Picoides albolarvatus* (Scientific) *Pic à tête blanche* (French; "white-headed woodpecker) *Carpintero cabeza blanca* (Spanish; "white-headed carpenter bird")

1

When I first saw White-headed Woodpeckers, I heard a small group of them (a family group, I guess) calling as they came into view. They reminded me of a little group of tree monkeys. I suppose that the distinct, dark eye against an all-white face and their acrobatic maneuvering gave me this odd idea.

### Identification

Medium-sized woodpecker with entirely black body and tail; face, throat, crown and wing patches white; males have a small red patch on the back of the head; the white head makes this species unmistakable.

### Sounds

Sharp *petek* call, rattle call extends from simple call.

Drum is long and variable, but generally medium tempo.

### Habitat

Montane pine forests; strong association with Ponderosa Pine, but most abundant where more than one pine species is common. Seeks mature pine forest with large cones and abundant seeds, open canopy and snags present for nest cavities.

### Range

Mountains of the far west, from British Columbia south through California; east to western Idaho and Nevada; range disjointed by rugged topography.

### Food

Mostly beetles, ants, and other arthropods found on trees; also seeds of pine trees. White-headed Woodpeckers take the seeds out of pine cones one by one, clinging (sometimes

1. Males show a bit of red behind the head.

# No Pounding Headache

Woodpeckers can spend much of the day chiseling out hard wood, flaking tough bark off tree trunks and pounding their bills against solid surfaces in rapid-fire patterns to communicate. How can they do this without pain and injury?

Woodpeckers have four features that allow them to handle the tremendous force caused by these activities: their beaks are strong but flexible, a layer of elastic tissue surrounds their tongues, they have spaces between their skulls and brains that dampen vibrations, and the bones in their head are spongy, not rigid. Like all birds, they are tougher than we may imagine.

Clinging acrobatically to a pine cone, this White-headed Woodpecker is prying seeds from between the scales.

upside down) to the large cones of the species they prefer, scoring the cones and, after breaking into the cone, plucking out the seed.

Non-migratory, but individuals do occasionally wander well away from usual range.

White-headeds are seen drinking from streams and puddles more often than other woodpeckers, possibly due to the higher presence of dry pine seeds in their diet.

While they spend much of their time slowly foraging their way up tree trunks, they periodically leap up to new spots, so when several are present, they may give the impression of swinging through the woods.

Both sexes work on nest site; eggs are white but may be stained with pine sap; clutch size averages four to five.

2. Excavating a nest cavity is dirty work; wood chips must be tossed out as the work progresses.

## Piercing Tongues

Woodpecker tongues are tough and "bony," lined with barbs or teeth and extend well beyond their bills; so a woodpecker can push its bill in a hole and then extend its tongue well beyond that into the wood. If the prey is a grub or other soft morsel, the hard tip of the tongue will pierce the prey, and the barbs will hold it on the tongue as the woodpecker retracts its tongue back into its mouth. The long tongue is then wrapped back up in a sheath around the inside of the skull.

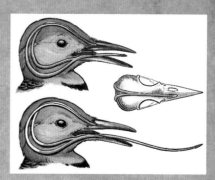

Woodpecker tongues are retractable, a very useful trait when feeding on insects deep inside a crevice. (Illustration by Denise Takahashi)

3. Large Ponderosa Pine provide cone seeds and nest sites.

4. Ponderosa Pine forest is their preferred habitat.

# Black-backed Woodpecker

*Description*  Glossy all-black back, heavy black-and-white barring on sides, male has crisp yellow cap

*Juveniles*  Similar to adult but duller, with crown patch (if any) reduced in size

*Length*  9.5 inches

*Wingspan*  15 inches

*Range*  Alaska, across Canada to treeline, south to northern Rocky Mountains, Black Hills, northern border states

*Other Names*  *Picoides arcticus* (Scientific)
Black-backed Three-toed Woodpecker
Arctic Three-toed Woodpecker
*Pic à dos noir* (French)
*El pájaro carpintero de espalda negra* (Spanish)

1

B lack-backed and American Three-toed Woodpeckers are residents of the far north or of mountainous areas. They differ from all other woodpeckers in their mostly-black plumage with no red, and in having three toes (two to the front, and one to the back) instead of four. These species have had their English names changed repeatedly as the research of the day has shifted them around the taxonomic landscape. One or the other has sometimes been Arctic Three-toed Woodpecker, or Northern Three-toed Woodpecker, or Black-backed Three-toed Woodpecker. Since 2006, they have been settled into their current names.

## Identification

Medium-sized woodpecker with solid glossy black, upper parts and white underparts barred with black on the sides and flanks; black-and-white barring in the underwings, white outer tail feathers, and white strip on the face. The male has a noticeable yellow patch in the center of the crown; not present in the female.

Distinguished from similar American Three-toed Woodpecker by all-dark upperparts, white outer tail feathers, more solid yellow crown patch in male.

## Sounds

Deep, pure call note; lower pitched and more metallic than Three-toed; aggressive, zippy rattle call, snarling with clicks.

2

Baby woodpeckers void wastes in fecal sacs, white membranes that encase fecal matter. This enables the adults to remove the waste easily and keep the nest hole clean.

The adults pick up the sac with their bill, and then, rather than just flinging it from the entrance, they fly out and drop the sac some distance from the nest tree (See photo on page 74). This helps confuse predators, which cannot discover nests just by looking for piles of fecal sacs.

Red-bellied Woodpeckers are an exception to this behavior; they leave the sacs in the nest, but cover them with new wood shavings they chisel from the inside walls of the cavity, keeping the babies clean and dry.

1. Note their glossy black sheen and male's yellow cap.

2. Black-backeds often remove a ring of bark around their nest hole.

Drums in faster, longer bursts than American Three-toed. Often detected by the sound of flaking bark.

## Habitat

Boreal and montane coniferous forests including bogs; often found in forests disturbed by fire, wind, or insect outbreak; less tied to wet spruce forests than Three-toed.

## Range

Alaska, across Canada to treeline, south to northern Rocky Mountains, Black Hills, northern border states; south into Sierras.

## Food

Mostly larvae of wood-boring beetles. May increase dramatically in areas infested with Eastern Larch Beetle or in recent burns.

Climbs on tree trunks, sometimes scrambles across downed logs, searching for beetles. Once a Black-backed finds a good supply of food, it may remain near that site for some time.

## Behavior Notes

Most often seen in disturbed conifers; most frequently found by searching for flaked bark and listening for quiet sounds of flaking.

Since it may overlap closely with American Three-toed Woodpecker in range and habitat, frequent agitated interactions occur; Black-backeds will chase Three-toeds away from prime areas. Both species may respond to the other's calls.

Selects nest sites in live and dead trees of a wide variety of species; both sexes excavate the nest and incubate; males incubate at night; average clutch size is three or four.

3. Black-backeds flake the bark off beetle-infested spruce and Tamarack to get at the grubs beneath.

4. Black Spruce and Tamarack bog habitat in the Sax-Zim Bog of northern Minnesota.

# Forest Fires & Woodpeckers

When a forest has burned, beetles are drawn to the area by the resins given off by the burnt wood. Once beetles become concentrated in a small area, even more beetles are attracted, and the number of beetles in a burn can become amazingly high. Any species of woodpecker can take advantage of this food supply, but Black-backed and American Three-toed Woodpeckers are especially attracted to burn areas.

Sometimes dozens of individuals of these two species will be found in a single burn. The Black-backeds will concentrate on the inner, more heavily charred trees, where they can use their larger size and robust bills to dig deeper into the wood. American Three-toeds will stay to the edges and less-charred trees.

Other disturbances in the forest, like an area of trees blown down or killed by an insect outbreak, can have a similar attraction to beetles and woodpeckers too.

# American Three-toed Woodpecker

**Description** Medium-sized, black woodpecker with white barring on the back and underparts, ragged yellow patch on the crown

**Juveniles** Similar to adults but plumage infused with buff and brown

**Length** 8.25 inches

**Wingspan** 15 inches

**Range** Across Canada and Alaska, south in the Rocky Mountains to New Mexico and Arizona and in the northern-most eastern United States

**Other Names** *Picoides dorsalis* (Scientific) northern three-toed woodpecker
*Pic tridactyle* (French)
*Carpintero de tres dedos* (Spanish)

1

B ecause it lives far from most humans and is uncommon even in its preferred haunts, many birders dream of finding this species. Formerly lumped with its close Eurasian relative as the only woodpecker found all around the Northern Hemisphere, but now split into two species—this species and the Eurasian Three-toed Woodpecker (*Picoides tridactylus*).

## Identification

Medium-sized, dark woodpecker with black on the sides, white underparts heavily barred with black, variable white markings on a black back, head mostly black with white chin and throat, yellow crown with ragged, whitish margin in both sexes (indistinct on female), white line from base of bill below eye; reddish-brown eye; three toes—two forward and one to the rear; sexes similar. Western birds are larger and have more extensive white on the back. See Black-backed Woodpecker and Yellow-bellied Sapsucker.

## Sounds

Call a low, soft *pik*, with a wooden quality; rattle call shorter than zippy call of Black-backed; almost always quieter than Black-backed; sometimes detected by the sound of flaking bark.

Drum is short, slow, accelerating and trailing off at the end.

2

American Three-toed Woodpeckers and Black-backed Woodpeckers have three toes; other woodpecker species have four. The mechanics of one fewer toe is thought to provide greater striking power but worse climbing ability.

On the charred bark in the areas preferred by these woodpeckers, perhaps climbing is difficult anyway, so the advantage of a fourth toe is smaller than it is for other woodpeckers.

Tridactyl is the term for animals with three toes (or any other body part). Zygodactyl refers to four-toed critters.

1. The yellow crown is unique to the males.

2. Female (no yellow cap) at nest cavity in an aspen.

## Habitat

Boreal and mountain forests that include insect-infested trees; stronger preference for spruce and wet forests than Black-backed; seeks out forests disturbed by fire, flood, or wind, where there are likely to be infestations of bark beetles.

## Range

Breeds farther north than any other woodpecker; range extends from Kodiak Island in the west through Alaska and across the forested areas of Canada to the Atlantic. In the United States, occurs uncommonly in the northern tier of states, and well south through the eastern Rockies to New Mexico and Arizona.

## Food

Mainly wood-boring beetle larvae, also caterpillars and other insects, some fruits and sap.

## Behavior Notes

Feeds by flaking the bark off trees in search of beetles and their larvae.

Does not migrate; however, irruptions occur, usually in response to changes in the food supply.

3. The vast boreal forest of Canada, Alaska and the northern Lower 48 is the primary habitat of the American Three-toed Woodpecker.

# Woodpecker Genera

There are four major genera (classifications) of woodpecker in North America. (Pileateds are the lone member of their genus) Sometimes the factors that scientists used to place these species in their groups were not primarily chosen according to the way the bird appears, so for birders, it is occasionally confusing. Nonetheless, thinking about which species belong to each group can be an enlightening step in learning about these birds:

**Genus *Melanerpes***—medium-sized woodpeckers that eat a varied diet:

Lewis's Woodpecker

Red-headed Woodpecker

Acorn Woodpecker

Gila Woodpecker

Golden-fronted Woodpecker

Red-bellied Woodpecker

**Genus *Sphyrapicus***—sapsuckers

Yellow-bellied Sapsucker

Red-naped Sapsucker

Red-breasted Sapsucker

Williamson's Sapsucker

**Genus *Picoides***—small- or mid-sized woodpeckers with black and white spots or patches:

Ladder-backed Woodpecker

Nuttall's Woodpecker

Downy Woodpecker

Hairy Woodpecker

Arizona Woodpecker

Red-cockaded Woodpecker

Black-backed Woodpecker

White-headed Woodpecker

Am. Three-toed Woodpecker

**Genus *Colaptes***—flickers

Northern Flicker

Gilded Flicker

# Northern Flicker

**Description** Brown barred back, white rump patch, spotted underparts with black bib; yellow or pinkish wing linings; male with red mustache

**Juveniles** Similar to adults

**Length** 12.5 inches

**Wingspan** 20 inches

**Range** One of the most widespread birds in North America, from the treeline in Alaska and Canada, across the entire lower 48 states, south into Mexico

**Other Names** *Colaptes auratus* (Scientific) high-hole, wake-up, pigeon woodpecker, harrywicket, yellowhammer
*Pic flamboyant* (French; "flamboyant woodpecker")
*Pic-palo lombricero* (Spanish)

1

**T**his is one of the most widespread bird species in North America, and it is a bird that people notice. Forbush wrote that there are over 100 common names for this species; some of the more interesting ones are high-hole, wake-up, pigeon woodpecker, yellowhammer, and harrywicket.

### Identification

Large gray-brown woodpecker with transverse dark-brown barring on back; off-white underparts with round spots and a large black crescent bib; conspicuous white rump patch; the underwing is either yellow (eastern) or pinkish-red (western); black (eastern) or red (western) mustache mark in males; Red-shafted has brown crown and nape with gray face; Yellow-shafted has gray crown, red nape and gray face.

Gilded Flicker is most similar to western, Red-shafted, but has more cinnamon in the crown, a larger black bib, paler upperparts and face, crescent-shaped spots on the underparts, and most noticeably, but only in flight, yellow wing linings.

### Sounds

High, piercing *kew*; loud series of *wik-a wik-a*

## Cavity Nesters

Over 80 species of vertebrates (animals with backbones, including birds) use cavities in trees for nesting and shelter. Sometimes cavities appear due to erosion in the wood or due to insect damage, but most usable tree cavities are made by woodpeckers. This makes the presence and health of woodpeckers essential in woodland ecosystems.

1. The red "mustache" marks this bird as the western form of the Northern Flicker—the "Red-shafted" Flicker.

notes; long *pik-pik-pik-pik* series, similar to but distinguishable from Pileated—Flicker is steady, maintains pitch, and ends abruptly, Pileated trails off and slows down at the end; the tone is different too but it takes practice to tell the difference.

2

## Habitat
Prefers open woodlands, forest edge, and savanna-like landscapes (grassy areas with well-spaced, large trees). The structure of the woodland is more important to this species than the species of trees.

## Range
From the treeline south in Alaska and Canada, across the entire lower 48 states, south into Mexico.

## Food
At least half the diet is comprised of ants, with the remainder consisting of beetles and other insects, along with various fruits and seeds.

## Behavior Notes
Northern Flicker has a proportionally thinner bill than other woodpeckers, and the bill is slightly curved. This fits with the flicker's life of foraging more by probing and catching ants than by chiseling wood.

Northern populations are migratory, moving to the southern United States, although some birds will linger late into the winter. Enormous flights are seen at migration counts in the fall.

3

---

2. Yellow-shafted form of the Northern Flicker emerges from its nest cavity with the young's fecal sacs.

3. Flickers are often seen on the ground foraging for ants.

# Yellow-shafted & Red-shafted Flickers

**P**rior to 1973, Yellow-shafted Flicker (mainly in the eastern U.S.) and Red-shafted Flicker (west of the Great Plains) were considered separate species. The striking difference in the color of their underwings made it seem obvious that they were two different species.

The American Ornithologist's Union combined the species when it was discovered how common hybridization was between the two; there is a wide swath of North America from Alaska to Texas where hybrids occur.

The hybrid flicker pictured here has the yellow tail feathers of a Yellow-shafted and the red mustache of a male Red-shafted.

"Yellow-shafted Flicker"

"Red-shafted Flicker"

Hybrid Flicker

# Gilded Flicker

**Description** Similar to other flickers, with brown back with faint black barring, white rump patch, cinnamon crown, red whisker stripe ("mustache"), yellow underwing

**Juveniles** Dull plumage similar to adults

**Length** 11.5 inches

**Wingspan** 18 inches

**Range** Southern Arizona, rare in California, south through Baja California and coastal Mexico

**Other Names** *Colaptes chrysoides* (Scientific)
*Pic chrysolide* (French)
*Carpintero aliamarillo, Carpintero de alas amarillas* (Spanish; "gold carpenter bird")

1

Like the other flickers, Gilded Flickers are conspicuous and widespread in their preferred habitat. They are a key ecological element of the Sonoran Desert. At middle elevations, they interbreed with Red-shafted Flickers.

## Identification
Big brown woodpecker with dark barring on the back, black bib, large white rump patch, yellow wing linings; differentiated from other flickers by brighter cinnamon-colored crown, no red on the back of the head, and especially by more extensive black on the underside of the tail.

## Sounds
Similar to Northern Flicker; high, piercing *kue*, also a series of *wucka, wucka, wucka*; song is steady, long *kuh,-kuh-kuh-kuh*, ending abruptly without descending or changing speed.

## Habitat
Strongly associated with giant cactus deserts at low elevations, but may also nest in cottonwood or willow lowlands.

## Range
Southern Arizona, rare in California, south through Baja California and coastal Mexico.

## Food
Ants, fruits, seeds and Saguaro cactus pollen.

## Behavior Notes
Nests usually within eight feet of the top of a Saguaro. Gilded Flickers are able to chisel through the tough cactus ribs and carve out a cavity. Gila Woodpeckers are smaller and need to make holes lower down on the Saguaro where they can excavate between the more widely spaced ribs.

1. Gilded Flickers love to feed on Saguaro cactus flower pollen.

# Flickers, Flickers, Everywhere

There are two species of flicker: Northern Flicker and Gilded Flicker, but there are also several subspecies of Northern Flicker, including a Guatemalan Flicker, a Cuban Flicker, which also occurs on Grand Cayman Island, and the Red-shafted Flicker of the western United States.

Flickers are found everywhere in North America, but they are also specialists; they need open woodlands and forest edges. They eat mostly ants, but also many other foods when need be. These characteristics make flickers well-suited for suburban and urban habitats.

A Saguaro makes a fine home for this nestling Gilded Flicker.

# Pileated Woodpecker

**Description** BIG woodpecker with a black body, large red crest, some white markings, and a large, chisel-shaped bill; as big as an average-sized crow

**Juveniles** Plumage similar to adults, but the feathers are less glossy and look scruffier; the red tones may appear more orange on younger birds

**Length** 16.5 inches

**Wingspan** 29 inches

**Range** Most of the Eastern U.S. and Southern Canada; south on West Coast to central California

**Other Names** *Dryocopus pileatus* (Scientific)
log cock, Indian rooster, rain crow, lord god bird
*Grand Pic* (French: "big woodpecker")
*Picamaderos Norteamericano* (Spanish)

When I was a boy, two Pileated Woodpeckers tore into a large cottonwood tree behind my grandparents' farmhouse. We'd hear the *chunk chunk* of their bills as they chiseled away at the tree, and in the morning we'd hear their wild, laughing calls. That tree was at least three feet in diameter, but it didn't take long for the woodpeckers to open gaping holes in the trunk. I was used to little birds picking at birdseed or chasing bugs or plucking berries, and the pure power and achievement of these Pileateds was impressive.

I haven't seen a more devastating woodpecker job since, but I still love to see and hear these woodpeckers. Most often I just hear them—their ringing calls sound like the jungle to my generation, because their calls were used in older movies that featured the jungle, even though these are not jungle birds. Seeing them is even more fun. Usually, I see them flying over the road; first, I'll think it's a crow, and then I'll catch the flash of white in the wings and the crest, laid back along the head.

Part of the allure of seeing and hearing Pileated Woodpeckers is their relative abundance. Pileateds are in the mid-range of bird species population density—on most days spent birding, you'll see one somewhere. However, when I have been asked to find one (for European birders, for example) the difficulty makes one realize that perhaps they aren't as common as it might seem. If there's a nest in your yard, of course, it's no problem; and they are large, conspicuous birds, so if they are around, you know it. Pileateds are a

# Tree Detectives

Woodpeckers run afoul of humans because sometimes the most attractive place for drilling for insects is the beautiful tree in your backyard. When someone sees the massive cavities Pileateds chisel into big old trees, it appears as if the woodpecker has destroyed a perfectly good tree.

"Appears" is the key word, however. Woodpeckers hold no grudge against trees. They are in search of food, and they make holes in wood to get at wood-boring insects (mainly Carpenter Ants and beetles).

However, in a twist worthy of a fictional crime story, the woodpeckers are not really the criminals—they're the crime-stoppers who do their best to stop the bad guys before the tree is reduced to sawdust. In other words, if the tree were in great shape, the woodpeckers would have no desire to go to the effort to dig holes in them. Their work may stop the damage, leaving the tree to live longer.

1

1. Carpenter Ant infestations in trees usually starts at the base, and this Pileated is performing contortions to get at them.

good example of what makes birding in general interesting. If all birds were as common and as easy to see as robins, there would be no game to searching for birds. If all birds were as tough to find as American Three-toed Woodpeckers, few would stick with it. Pileateds are on the common end of this spectrum; and they are a species that is noticed and enjoyed by lots of people who aren't even aware of other kinds of woodpeckers.

## Identification

Pileated Woodpecker is the largest woodpecker in North America (but see the Ivory-billed Woodpecker sidebar on pg. 85). Its most recognizable field marks are its large black body and red crest; big, chisel-shaped bill; broad white wing linings are obvious in flight and give a distant, flying Pileated the appearance of "flashing" as it flies.

The eyes are light-colored, a black eyeline extends back to the nape of the neck, and a broad white stripe extends from the bill along the sides of the head and neck and then down toward the wings.

Males are red from the forehead to the red crest, and the mustache is red in front and black toward the back. Females have entirely black mustaches and are black or buff-colored on the forehead.

## Sounds

Long, variable *kik kik kik kik kik* ; louder, less even, slower, and with a more hollow quality than Northern Flicker calls, which are similar; this call trails off and descends at the end; flicker calls end abruptly.

Their drumming is often loud and resonant, due to their power, and to their use of resonant places to drum. I once saw and heard a Pileated drumming on a large metal electrical tower along the Mississippi River; it was loud! Drums come in continuous rolls, followed by one or two loud taps.

---

2. Many woodpeckers have an up-and-down undulating flight pattern, but Pileateds fly in a fairly straight trajectory (Composite image of nine consecutive flight shots).

When they are excavating, their blows are loud, slow beats. If you imitate this sound (using a stick on a tree, or even clapping your hands), the birds will sometimes come closer to get a look at you.

### Habitat

Across their range, Pileateds can be found wherever there are trees with big trunks; they will also use younger forests, provided there are at least some large-diameter trees present. They will use both deciduous and coniferous tree; they also prefer closed canopy forests and sites near water.

### Range

Widespread across the mature, northern forest of North America, especially in the East; from Nova Scotia to southern Florida and west to the Mississippi River throughout the eastern United States. In Canada, their range extends all the way across the country to the Pacific Ocean. Their range also extends south along the West Coast and into the northern Sierras and Rockies.

3. Pileateds can really tear into a tree heavily infested with Carpenter Ants. Large rectangular holes are characteristic of the Pileated.

# Recycled Housing

**M**any woodpeckers do not reuse nest cavities from one year to the next. But their excavation efforts do not go to waste. Many critters including other birds (owls, kestrels, ducks) and mammals (flying squirrels, marten, squirrels) use them for nesting and roosting.

From top left, clockwise—1. Northern Pygmy-Owl peeks out from a Hairy Woodpecker cavity. 2. Juvenile Northern Saw-whet Owl in a Northern Flicker cavity. 3. Female American Kestrel also utilizing a Flicker hole. 4. Flammulated Owl nesting in discarded Flicker nest cavity. 5. Not just birds! Five Flying Squirrels cluster at entrance to old Pileated Woodpecker hole. 6. Western Bluebird finds a cozy home in a former nest of a Hairy Woodpecker.

### Food

They love to eat Carpenter Ants and wood-boring beetles, along with a wide variety of other bugs, also fruits and nut. They forage on many tree species across their range, but everywhere they prefer large, older trees. Studies have shown them to spend two-thirds of their time on dead trees, and even for living trees, they spend over ninety percent of their time on dead wood.

Their banging on trees not only chips away wood, but the noise and commotion causes any ants present to move, making them easier to harvest.

### Behavior Notes

Pileated Woodpeckers usually mate for life. They will often stay within the same territory, so long as the food source persists. Their courtship displays include flapping their wings, waving their bills, and raising their crests. They protect their territory through drumming, calling, and chasing intruders.

Over ninety-five percent of the time, they choose trees for nesting that were already hollow from decay, rather than from excavation; so the woodpeckers only have to excavate entrance holes. They often

4

4. Pileated pair; male (lower bird) sports a red "mustache," while female above lacks this mark.

# Empty Nest Syndrome

Most of the year, I don't see or hear Pileated Woodpeckers around my house. Almost every February, however, I catch a glimpse of a Pileated on the dead stump (about six feet high) that I keep intact in my front yard. I assume that these are different birds, and that they are young individuals who have been chased out of their birth territories.

Pileated Woodpeckers don't migrate; they often just stay in the same patches of woods for most of their lives. When young birds mature, they need to leave their home territory and find another, either a suitable place where there are no other Pileated Woodpeckers, or where they find a mate who has lost its prior partner. This reshuffling of territories usually happens in late winter or early spring, so that's a good time to keep your eyes open for Pileated Woodpeckers on the move.

# Baby, It's Cold Outside!

Most woodpeckers do not migrate, so northern species end up dealing with bitterly cold conditions during the winter. They compensate by consuming more food, by using cavities for roosting, and by piloerection, which means extending their feathers out from their body. Small muscles beneath the skin contract when the bird is cold, and this causes the feathers to stand away from the bird's body at a wider angle. This creates more air space around the feathers and provides more insulation against the cold. Mammals have a similar mechanism for their fur; human mammals get goose bumps!

Pileated using piloerection to stay warm at Minus 25 F in northern Minnesota.

make multiple entrances (up to sixteen!) so they can escape easily if a predator enters the tree. Pileateds also roost in hollow trees at night and during bad weather.

Pileated Woodpeckers are great at flying and great at moving up and down vertical tree trunks. They can walk and hop if necessary, but they aren't very good at either.

5

Carpenter Ants are the preferred food of the Pileated; and since the infestation often starts near the tree's base, that is where you may see the initial excavations. In this split log you can see where a Pileated chiseled in to access the Carpenter Ant galleries (vertical burrows).

5. Female leaves her nest cavity in an aspen.

# Ivory-billed Woodpecker

Another large, crested woodpecker once lived in North America, the Ivory-billed Woodpecker (*Campephilus principalis*). The Ivory-billed was even larger than Pileated Woodpecker, plus it had a flattened bill tip, white streaks on the back, and broad white sections on the leading and trailing edges of the wings. Ivory-billeds lacked the white facial-markings of Pileateds, and their calls were nasal and quite distinct.

This species lived in mature forests in the southeastern United States. Its numbers were severely reduced through the nineteenth century by logging and collection for feathers. Finally, there were just

a few left in Louisiana, and once their woods were clear-cut, they vanished. The last certain photographs taken in the United States are from 1938. The last confirmed photos of the species were taken in Cuba (which may ultimately be considered a separate species) in 1948. The last authenticated reports of Cuban birds were in 1987.

In the decades since, there have been several tantalizing reports from Cuba, Arkansas, Louisiana and Florida. Controversy surrounds all of these reports, photos and videos, and none are universally accepted as Ivory-billed Woodpeckers. Search efforts in the areas where the reports came from failed to generate any further evidence; the Ivory-billed Woodpecker is, alas, still extinct.

1918 Arm & Hammer Baking Soda trading card, "Useful Birds of America" Second Series #21
"...Once a common bird of the southern states, it is much to be deplored that this fine woodpecker is now threatened with extinction. No other bird can get at the destructive wood-boring grubs which the Ivory-bill destroys in great numbers."

# Bibliography

Aubry, Keith B. and Catherine M. Raley. 2002. *The Pileated Woodpecker as a Keystone Habitat Modifier in the Pacific Northwest.* USDA Forest Service Gen. Tech. Rep. PSW-GTR-181.

Baicich, Paul J. and Colin J.O. Harrison. 1997. *A Guide to the Nests, Eggs, and Nestlings of North American Birds* (2nd ed.). San Diego: Academic Press.

Bannick, Paul. 2008. *The Owl and the Woodpecker: Encounters with North America's Most Iconic Birds.* Seattle: Mountaineers.

Benson, David R. 2008. *Owls of the North: a Naturalist's Handbook.* Duluth: Stone Ridge Press.

Bent, A. C. 1939. *Life Histories of North American Woodpeckers.* U.S. Natl. Mus. Bull. no. 174.

Bull, Evelyn L. and Jerome A. Jackson. 1995. *Pileated Woodpecker (Dryocopus pileatus), The Birds of North America Online* (A. Poole, Ed.). Ithaca: Cornell Lab of Ornithology; Retrieved from the *Birds of North America Online*: http://bna.birds.cornell.edu/bna/species/148 doi:10.2173/bna.148

Chapman, F. M. 1939. *Handbook of Birds of Eastern North America.* D. Appleton-Century Co. New York.

Dixon, Rita D. and Victoria A. Saab. 2000. *Black-backed Woodpecker (Picoides arcticus), The Birds of North America Online* (A. Poole, Ed.). Ithaca: Cornell Lab of Ornithology; Retrieved from the *Birds of North America* Online: http://bna.birds.cornell.edu/bna/species/509 doi:10.2173/bna.509

Dunn, Jon L. and Jonathan Alderfer, eds. 2011. *National Geographic Field Guide to the Birds of North America* (Sixth Edition). Washington, DC: National Geographic Society.

Eckert: Kim R. 2002. *A Birder's Guide to Minnesota* (4th ed.). Duluth: Gavian.

Edwards, Holly H. and Gary D. Schnell. 2000. *Gila Woodpecker (Melanerpes uropygialis), The Birds of North America Online* (A.

Poole, Ed.). Ithaca: Cornell Lab of Ornithology; Retrieved from the *Birds of North America Online*: http://bna.birds.cornell.edu/bna/species/532 doi:10.2173/bna.532

Ehrlich, Paul, David Dobkin, and D. Wheye. 1988. *The Birder's Handbook: a Field Guide to the Life Histories of North American Birds.* New York: Simon & Schuster.

Elbroch, Mark and Eleanor Marks. 2001. *Bird Tracks and Sign: A Guide to North American Species.* Pennsylvania: Stackpole.

Ellison, W. G. 1992. *Identifying the rhythms of northeastern woodpeckers.* Birding 24:351-354.

Erickson, Laura. 1993. *For the Birds: An Uncommon Guide.* Minneapolis: University of Minnesota.

Farrand, John, Jr, ed. 1983. *The Audubon Society Master Guide to Birding,* vol. 2. New York: Knopf.

Forbush, Edward Howe, and John Richard May, rev. 1955. *A Natural History of American Birds of Eastern and Central North America.* New York: Bramhall House.

Garrett, Kimball L., Martin G. Raphael and Rita D. Dixon. 1996. *White-headed Woodpecker (Picoides albolarvatus), The Birds of North America Online* (A. Poole, Ed.). Ithaca: Cornell Lab of Ornithology; Retrieved from the *Birds of North America* Online: http://bna.birds.cornell.edu/bna/species/252 doi:10.2173/bna.252

Godfrey, W. E. 1986. *The Birds of Canada.* Rev. ed. Natl. Mus. Nat. Sci. Ottawa.

Goodwin, D. 1968. *Notes on Woodpeckers (Picidae).* Bulletin of the British Museum (Natural History) Zoology Volume 17 No. 1. London.

Green, Janet C. 1995. *Birds in Forests: A Management and Conservation Guide.* St. Paul, MN: Minnesota Department of Natural Resources.

# Bibliography

Gyug, Les W., R. C. Dobbs, T. E. Martin and C. J. Conway. 2012. *Williamson's Sapsucker (Sphyrapicus thyroideus), The Birds of North America Online* (A. Poole, Ed.). Ithaca: Cornell Lab of Ornithology; Retrieved from the *Birds of North America Online*: http://bna.birds.cornell.edu/bna/species/285 doi:10.2173/bna.285

Husak, Michael S. and Terry C. Maxwell. 1998. *Golden-fronted Woodpecker (Melanerpes aurifrons), The Birds of North America Online* (A. Poole, Ed.). Ithaca: Cornell Lab of Ornithology; Retrieved from the *Birds of North America Online*: http://bna.birds.cornell.edu/bna/species/373 doi:10.2173/bna.373

Icenoggle, Radd. 2003. *Birds in Place: A Habitat-based Field Guide to Birds of the Northern Rockies*. Helena: Farcountry Press.

Jackson, Jerome A. 1994. *Red-cockaded Woodpecker (Picoides borealis), The Birds of North America Online* (A. Poole, Ed.). Ithaca: Cornell Lab of Ornithology; Retrieved from the *Birds of North America Online*: http://bna.birds.cornell.edu/bna/species/085 doi:10.2173/bna.85

Jackson, Jerome A. 2002. *Ivory-billed Woodpecker (Campephilus principalis), The Birds of North America Online* (A. Poole, Ed.). Ithaca: Cornell Lab of Ornithology; Retrieved from the *Birds of North America Online*: http://bna.birds.cornell.edu/bna/species/711 doi:10.2173/bna.711

Jackson, Jerome A. and Henri R. Ouellet. 2002. *Downy Woodpecker (Picoides pubescens), The Birds of North America Online* (A. Poole, Ed.). Ithaca: Cornell Lab of Ornithology; Retrieved from the *Birds of North America Online*: http://bna.birds.cornell.edu/bna/species/613 doi:10.2173/bna.613

Jackson, Jerome A., Henri R. Ouellet and Bette J. Jackson. 2002. *Hairy Woodpecker (Picoides villosus), The Birds of North America Online* (A. Poole, Ed.). Ithaca: Cornell Lab of Ornithology; Retrieved from the *Birds of North America Online*: http://bna.birds.cornell.edu/bna/species/702 doi:10.2173/bna.702

Johnson, R. Roy, Lois T. Haight and J. David Ligon. 1999. *Arizona Woodpecker (Picoides arizonae), The Birds of North America Online* (A. Poole, Ed.). Ithaca: Cornell Lab of Ornithology; Retrieved from the *Birds of North America Online*: http://bna.birds.cornell.edu/bna/species/474 doi:10.2173/bna.474

Kaufman, Kenn. 2011. *Field Guide to Advanced Birding*. Boston: Houghton Mifflin.

Kaufman, Kenn. 1996. *Lives of North American Birds*. Boston: Houghton Mifflin.

Kaufman, Kenn. 2000. *Birds of North America*. New York: Houghton Mifflin.

Kilham, Lawrence. 1992. *Woodpeckers of Eastern North America*. New York: Dover. Reprint of *Life History Studies of Woodpeckers of Eastern North America*. 1983. Cambridge, MA: Nuttall Ornithological Club.

Kilham, Lawrence. 1988. "Woodpeckers North and South," pp. 32-50 in *On Watching Birds*. Chelsea Green, Chelsea, Vermont.

Kline, David. 1990. *Great Possessions: An Amish Farmer's Journal*. San Francisco: North Point.

Koenig, Walter D., Peter B. Stacey, Mark T. Stanback and Ronald L. Mumme. 1995. *Acorn Woodpecker (Melanerpes formicivorus), The Birds of North America Online* (A. Poole, Ed.). Ithaca: Cornell Lab of Ornithology; Retrieved from the *Birds of North America Online*: http://bna.birds.cornell.edu/bna/species/194 doi:10.2173/bna.194

Leonard, Jr., David L. 2001. *American Three-toed Woodpecker (Picoides dorsalis), The Birds of North America Online* (A. Poole, Ed.). Ithaca: Cornell Lab of Ornithology; Retrieved from the *Birds of North America Online*: http://bna.birds.cornell.edu/bna/species/588 doi:10.2173/bna.588

# Bibliography

Lowther, Peter E. 2000. *Nuttall's Woodpecker (Picoides nuttallii), The Birds of North America Online* (A. Poole, Ed.). Ithaca: Cornell Lab of Ornithology; Retrieved from the *Birds of North America Online*: http://bna.birds.cornell.edu/bna/species/555 doi:10.2173/bna.555

Lowther, Peter E. 2001. *Ladder-backed Woodpecker (Picoides scalaris), The Birds of North America Online* (A. Poole, Ed.). Ithaca: Cornell Lab of Ornithology; Retrieved from the *Birds of North America Online*: http://bna.birds.cornell.edu/bna/species/565 doi:10.2173/bna.565

Lukes, Roy. 1979. *Out on a Limb: A Journal of Wisconsin Birding.* Bailey's Harbor, WI: Pine Street Press.

Marks, Paul. 2011. *Woodpecker's head inspires shock absorbers.* New Scientist 209 (2798):21.

Moore, William S. 1995. *Gilded Flicker (Colaptes chrysoides), The Birds of North America Online* (A. Poole, Ed.). Ithaca: Cornell Lab of Ornithology; Retrieved from the *Birds of North America Online*: http://bna.birds.cornell.edu/bna/species/166b doi:10.2173/bna.166

Nachtrier, Henry F. and P. L. Hatch. 1892. *Notes on the Birds of Minnesota.* Minneapolis: Harbison and Smith.

Nehrling, Henry. 1896. *Our Native Birds of Song and Beauty*, Vol. II. Milwaukee: George Brumder.

Pielou, E.C. 1988. *The World of Northern Evergreens.* Ithaca: Cornell.

Phillips, Steven J. and Patricia Wentworth Comus, eds., 2000. *A Natural History of the Sonoran Desert.* Tucson: Arizona-Sonora Desert Museum.

Ritchison, Gary. 1999. *Downy Woodpecker.* PA: Stackpole.

Roberts, Thomas S. 1932. *Birds of Minnesota.* Minneapolis: University of Minnesota.

Shackelford, Clifford E., Raymond E. Brown and Richard N. Conner. 2000. *Red-bellied Woodpecker (Melanerpes carolinus), The Birds of North America Online* (A. Poole, Ed.). Ithaca: Cornell Lab of Ornithology; Retrieved from the *Birds of North America Online*: http://bna.birds.cornell.edu/bna/species/500 doi:10.2173/bna.500

Short. Lester L. *Habits and Interactions of North American Three-toed Woodpeckers (Picoides arcticus and Picoides tridactylus). American Museum Novitates, Number 2547.* September 29, 1974. New York: American Museum of Natural History.

Short, L. L. 1982. *Woodpeckers of the World.* Delaware Mus. Nat. Hist. Monogr. no. 4.

Shunk, Stephen A. 2005. *Sphyrapicus Anxiety: Identifying Hybrid Sapsuckers.* pp. 289-298. Birding, May/June

Sibley, David Allen. 2000. *The Sibley Guide to Birds.* New York: Random House.

Sibley, David Allen. 2001. *The Sibley Guide to Bird Life and Behavior.* New York: Knopf.

Skutch, Alexander F. 1985. *Life of the Woodpecker.* Santa Monica, CA: Ibis.

Smith, Kimberly G., James H. Withgott and Paul G. Rodewald. 2000. *Red-headed Woodpecker (Melanerpes erythrocephalus), The Birds of North America Online* (A. Poole, Ed.). Ithaca: Cornell Lab of Ornithology; Retrieved from the *Birds of North America Online*: http://bna.birds.cornell.edu/bna/species/518doi:10.2173/bna.518

Stensaas, Mark. 1993. *Canoe Country Wildlife: A Field Guide to the Boundary Waters and Quetico.* Minneapolis: University of Minnesota.

Vierling, Kerri T., Victoria A. Saab and Bret W. Tobalske. 2013. *Lewis's Woodpecker (Melanerpes lewis), The Birds of North America Online* (A. Poole, Ed.). Ithaca: Cornell Lab of Ornithology; Retrieved from the *Birds of North America Online*: http://bna.birds.cornell.edu/bna/species/284doi:10.2173/bna.284

Walters, Eric L., Edward H. Miller and Peter E. Lowther. 2002. *Yellow-bellied Sapsucker (Sphyrapicus varius), The Birds of North America Online* (A. Poole, Ed.). Ithaca: Cornell Lab of Ornithology; Retrieved from the *Birds of North America Online*: http://bna.birds.cornell.edu/bna/species/662doi:10.2173/bna.662

Walters, Eric L., Edward H. Miller and Peter E. Lowther. 2002. *Red-breasted Sapsucker (Sphyrapicus ruber), The Birds of North America Online* (A. Poole, Ed.). Ithaca: Cornell Lab of Ornithology;

Retrieved from the *Birds of North America Online*:
http://bna.birds.cornell.edu/bna/species/663adoi:10.2173/bna.663

Walters, Eric L., Edward H. Miller and Peter E. Lowther. 2002. *Red-naped Sapsucker (Sphyrapicus nuchalis), The Birds of North America Online* (A. Poole, Ed.). Ithaca: Cornell Lab of Ornithology; Retrieved from the *Birds of North America Online*:
http://bna.birds.cornell.edu/bna/species/663bdoi:10.2173/bna.663

Weber, Larry. 2014. *Backyard Almanac.* Wrenshall, MN: Stone Ridge Press.

Wiebe, Karen L. and William S. Moore. 2008. *Northern Flicker (Colaptes auratus), The Birds of North America Online* (A. Poole, Ed.).

Ithaca: Cornell Lab of Ornithology; Retrieved from the *Birds of North America Online*:
http://bna.birds.cornell.edu/bna/species/166adoi:10.2173/bna.166

Williams, Jim and Anthony Hertzel. 2001. *Questions and Answers About Backyard Birds.* Cambridge, MN: Adventure.

Winkler, Hans, David A. Christie, and David Nurney. 1995. *Woodpeckers: a Guide to the Woodpeckers of the World.* Boston: Houghton Mifflin.

Zickefoose, Julie. March 10, 2009. *Woody the Acorn (not Pileated) Woodpecker.* All Things Considered (radio program) Retrieved from http://www.npr.org

# Photo Credits

All photos in the book are by Paul Bannick except those noted below. If we added up all the hours Paul spent in the field to get the photos in this book, the number would be staggering. Not to mention the conditions he endured—cramped blinds, soggy feet, blood-thirsty mosquitoes, finger-numbing cold. But the results are spectacular! See more of Paul's work at www.PaulBannick.com.

Carolyn Ohl (http://cmoasis.blogspot.com/): pg. 41 sidebar photos
Howard Rowe: pg. 24 bottom
Sparky Stensaas (www.ThePhotoNaturalist.com): pg. 20 top left, 21 sidebar photos, 25 all, 29 sidebar, 31, 32, 33 center, 48, 49 sidebar, 66 left, 79, 80 top, 81, 84 sidebar, 84 bottom
Paul Sundberg (www.paulsundbergphotography.com): pg. 82 bottom center
Larry Weber: pg. 49 left
Jim Williams (Google "wingnut startribune blog"): pg. 9 sidebar photos
Public Domain: pg. 5 sidebar top [Meriwether Lewis by Charles Wilson Peale via Wikimedia Commons], pg. 45 sidebar right [Flicker page scan via Archive.org], sidebar left [Thomas Nuttall presumably by Bass Otis via Wikimedia Commons]

# Index

# Index

# Also from Stone Ridge Press...

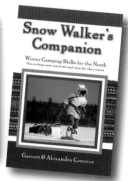

 more at www.stoneridgepress.com